The Egg-Free Cookbook

Get Back the Foods You've Been Missing

Tabitha Elliott

Cover Design by Mindy Van Gundy

© 2014 Little Things Books

Little Things Books

The Egg-Free Cookbook
Copyright © 2014 by Tabitha Elliott

Requests for information should be addressed to littlethingsbooks@gmail.com.

_____

Library of Congress Cataloging-in-Publication Data

Elliott, Tabitha A 1975-

    The egg-free cookbook: get back the foods you've been missing / Tabitha Elliott.

ISBN 978-0-615-56920-8 (softcover)   3

1. Cooking-Health & Healing-Allergy.

_____

Front cover design: Mindy Van Gundy

Dedication

To my "guinea pigs": Brian, Shealee, Jordan, Blade and Braxton.

Thank you for eating multiple batches of each recipe until I got it just right, laughing with me in the kitchen at first attempts at a new recipes gone horribly wrong, answering dozens of questions like, "does this taste like regular mayonnaise?... white cake? ... potato salad?", never complaining about modifying your diet for my sake (of course I know you didn't really care if your pancakes and French silk pie had eggs in it as long as it tasted yummy), and oh yes-for doing the dishes.

Cross Contamination
Warning & Disclaimer

It is the user's responsibility to verify that each ingredient they use for these recipes does not contain any form of eggs. Some types of food, such as bread crumbs, may or may not contain eggs depending on the brand.

Proper washing of cookware, dishes, cooking and surfaces must be completed to prevent cross-contamination from eggs or egg-containing food in the kitchen. Separate utensils must be used while preparing and serving these dishes alongside egg-containing foods.

The publisher and author are not responsible for any actions taken by readers or any adverse reactions that may result. This book is not intended to replace medical advice.

Reader Input Requested

Replacing eggs in every product and recipe in your kitchen can seem like a daunting task at the outset. This cookbook is the result of one woman's successful quest to do so.

The author hopes that this cookbook will make your journey far easier and less time consuming for you than it was for her. She would also love to hear about your results: your struggles and successes, and especially your input on how to improve any of the recipes.

Please visit Facebook.com/EggFreeCookbook for recipe updates or email the author at littlethings-books@gmail.com. Your suggestions or corrections may help make the journey easier for other individuals as well.

Posting or Sharing Recipes Online

The author has posted several selected recipes from the book online. Readers are encouraged to share these recipes directly from the author's various pages (Facebook.com/EggFreeCookbook, AllRecipes.com, etc.) and to make comments about this cookbook online.

Posting additional recipes from this cookbook, except for sharing links to what the author has already posted online, should not be done without permission as they are protected by copyright.

You are welcome to request permission to share an additional recipe online by emailing littlethings-books@gmail.com with the name of the recipe you wish to share and a link to the website where you wish to share it.

Table of Contents

Living with an

Egg Allergy

Foods that Typically Contain Eggs

Most baked goods:

Cookies, cakes, bars, banana bread

Most breakfast foods:

Pancakes, French toast, waffles, muffins

Anything with mayo:

Coleslaw, potato salad, tuna sandwich

Most white salad dressings:

Ranch, blue cheese, Caesar

Breaded and deep fried foods:

Fried chicken, appetizers

Many Desserts:

Cream pies, cheesecake, some puddings

Some Breads:

Dinner rolls, bakery breads (if coated in egg wash for shine)

This is not a complete list. Also, some commercially prepared foods may or may not contain eggs when made-from-scratch recipes do. Checking at one restaurant or on one package and finding out something is OK, does not mean the same food from another restaurant or brand will be the same. Check every place, every time.

Surprising Foods that Contain Eggs

Snickers® Bars

Milky Way® Bars

KFC® Extra Crispy Chicken

Wendy's® chicken sandwich patty

Chicken noodle soup

Fettuccini Alfredo

Lasagna

Corndogs

Sweet potato casserole

Some protein bars and drinks

Salt Water Taffey

Marshmallow crème

Some cake frosting

"Homestyle" vanilla ice cream, frozen custard

Candied nuts (sometimes served on salads)

My Story: A Note from the Author

A few years ago I was having some pretty rotten physical problems. I discovered through a simple and free test I did at home, that a lot of my symptoms occurred in the hours right after I ate anything that contained eggs. Since eggs are used in a wide variety of foods, I usually had a dose several times a day. Once I tested to see if I had a sensitivity to eggs it became very obvious that eggs had been knocking me down-and possibly for years!

It took me until my early 30's to discover that eggs were a problem for me. In high school doctors had been unable to determine what was causing me to have episodes of a racing heart beat, although they had ruled out a heart condition. In my 20's I began to struggle with fatigue and intermittent brain fog. I never suspected a food sensitivity could be the source of these problems until I picked up a book about food allergies one day at the age of 30.

The book explained how to do a simple preliminary test for food sensitivities at home. What captured my attention was their suggestion to start by seeing if a food would cause you to have a change in heart rate! To do this test, count your resting heart rate (sit and relax for 5 minutes prior to testing). Count for a full minute because a precise result will be important. Then eat the food you want to test. Take your *resting* pulse again 30, 60 and 90 minutes later. If your pulse jumps or slows down by more than 8 points, it's a sign that you may be sensitive to that food. My pulse jumped by 20 points after eating eggs!

To verify a food allergy, there are several testing methods. One standard method is the temporary use of an elimination diet. The person must completely avoiding all forms of the suspect food for 2-3 weeks. They then eat a portion of the food to see if it triggers any symptoms (*this should never be attempted by someone who has ever suffered a severe allergic reaction to a food except for under the guidance of a physician*).

After abstaining completely from anything that contained eggs for two weeks, I sat down to do the test. I ate 2 fried eggs. The bad news was I reacted; BAD! The good news was I finally had something I could do about my symptoms. Banish eggs from my life in all forms and get my full health back.

I went off eggs completely cold turkey-or should I say cold chicken? That meant I could no longer eat at least half of the foods I used to eat on a regular basis. It meant checking the ingredients on *everything* before I ate *anything*: at home, at restaurants, at catered events, and-the most difficult-at "buffet" style social events like potlucks and parties.

Once I rigorously avoided everything that contained eggs, any accidental exposure would cause a severe reaction. People with food intolerances often become more sensitive once they completely eliminate the offending food, but their health improves overall-often dramatically.

My family saw me fall prey to an accidental sneak egg attack a few times during the first few years while I was learning how to avoid eggs. Usually it was from some harmless looking food (such as a candy bar with nugget), or before I knew better than to trust waitresses who sound confident they knew the item I asked about on the menu didn't contain eggs, or by discovering that an entree made egg-free at the stove isn't egg-free at the table after you cross spatulas with the one you used to flip the kids' French toast.

Once, when I was starting to slur my words and make sensical non-sentences (comments just like the one I just made), my daughter stopped me and asked me, "Mommy, is your brain on eggs?" Remember the old T.V. commercial where an egg was frying in a pan and the announcer said in a deep voice, "This is your brain on drugs"? Well there were times when my brain fog was so bad due to eggs that I felt impaired by some kind of substance. But it wasn't crack cocaine, it was cracked-an-egg at breakfast.

Overcoming my egg addiction was a real challenge at first. Most people don't realize how many things contain eggs. I quickly found that waiters and waitresses often didn't have a clue and wouldn't take the time to go get one in the kitchen either unless prodded emphatically. Asking at a drive through window was a completely pointless exercise. Treats brought to the office, church potlucks, dinners at friends, and open salad bars all became risky ventures that could ruin the rest of my day. Telling people I didn't want any of their birthday cake, wedding cake, or their famous seven layer salad were all opportunities to be put in a socially awkward situation. Catered lunches, bakeries, and-the most dreaded dining establishments of all-waffle houses, could occasionally leave only a few things that were obviously safe to eat.

Cooking at home was easy by comparison. At least at home I got to choose what to cook and could read the labels so I knew it was safe. Well, at least it was after my family learned not to share my serving spoons, or put pots that came out of the dishwasher with a little yellow still stuck on them back in the cabinet, and to be careful where they crack eggs so they don't drizzle a little egg white on the stove where I could set down a spoon in the same place right behind them.

After a while, I got tired of having to skip over half of my cookbook. I missed the cookies, muffins, fried chicken, potato salad, breakfast foods and so many other foods I had grown up with. So, I drove to the next county to find a health food store that sold some kind of egg alternative mystery powder. It worked alright for some baked goods, but nothing else. It also was a real pain to mix.

Eventually I tossed the box and started looking for ways to recreate my favorite recipes one by one. It took years of experimentation, but the results were worth it. Now there isn't hardly anything I can't make, and I don't need to go further than my regular grocery store down the street for ingredients.

My hope is that this cookbook will become a source of freedom for you and your loved ones or guests with an egg allergy, and that you will enjoy your time cooking and the great food to follow.

- Tabitha

Everyday Living Guide

Here are a couple of important tips for living with an egg allergy.

Ingredient Labels: The summary of allergens a food contains is often listed at the bottom of the ingredients label. It can be helpful for quickly spotting that something contains eggs, but it is not always present or accurate. I have seen packages that contained egg products where eggs were not listed in the allergen summary. Always read the full ingredient list to verify.

Eating Out: Wait staff at restaurants often assume that if eggs aren't listed in the description on the menu, such as in a chef salad, that it doesn't have eggs. Do NOT take their initial advice. Always ask them to confirm with the kitchen, or better yet, to provide you with a written allergen guide.

If you wish to be discrete or minimize delays, arrive early and check the menu before your friends or business associates arrive. Ask the wait staff to confirm with the chef that what you wish to order is safe for you. Many restaurants now post their menus online, so it is possible to review it in advance and call the restaurant to check before arriving.

You might also consider filling out a small card (or print business cards) that explain you have an egg allergy, and ask the chef confirm that what you have ordered is safe for you to eat, and to prevent cross-contamination. Ask the waiter to give it to the chef.

Desserts are often the most difficult item to find egg-free at a restaurant. If nothing is safe on the dessert menu and you would like something sweet to finish off your meal, it is often acceptable at fine dining establishments to ask for fresh fruit, even if it is not on the menu. If any desserts are served al a mode, you could ask for a scoop of ice cream, if they verify it is egg-free. You could also order a specialty drink, such as a mocha coffee with whipped cream.

Fast Food Chains: Most are supposed to have allergen menus available, but sometimes they are hard to locate. They may be under the counter, posted on the wall, or available online. Find or print a copy off the internet and keep it on hand, such as in the glove compartment in your car, in order to help speed up trips to the counter or the drive-thru. Many burgers and sandwiches (including some chicken sandwiches) can be made egg-free by ordering it with a request to "hold the mayo". Asking for extra mustard and ketchup can help boost the flavor and replace the moisture missing from mayonnaise.

Sub Shops: Sandwiches of all types can often be made egg-free by leaving off the mayo. They may make your sub sandwich with foods that are safe for you to eat, but unless you ask them to change their gloves and wash their knife first, they might slice a line of egg-rich mayo into your egg-free sandwich. Let them know you have an egg allergy and ask them to use a fresh work surface and knife. Most employees are happy to do so when they know the request is due to a food allergy.

Potlucks/Parties: Potlucks are notorious for mayonnaise-laden foods. This makes every creamy dish off limits unless the cook is nearby and can remember what it contains. Compliment the dish— "Oh, that looks good! Who made it?" Once you identify the maker, then you can ask that person, "That looks great! What's in it?"

I've found it is very useful to ask, **"Does it contain any eggs _or mayonnaise_?"**, because few people remember that mayo is made from eggs and oil and it is a common used ingredient in many side-dishes.

When invited to a potluck or picnic, volunteer to bring something that usually contains eggs, such as potato salad. This guarantees there will be at least one variety that you know is safe. Plus, if other cooks know that you will be bringing that item, they are more likely to bring something else. You might luck out if they bring something that you can actually eat instead, like baked beans.

People sometimes respond that they feel bad that you can't eat something they made. I always reassure them, "No, it's ok! I just appreciate knowing what I can and can't eat! I can find plenty of things I can eat."

School Treats: Have the teacher send out a notice to the parents saying there is a child in the classroom with an egg allergy. This is now common so there will likely be other children in the school with a food allergy. Ask the teacher to check with parents each time treats are brought to the classroom to see if they contain eggs as they will likely forget it is an issue. Keep a stash of pre-packaged treats with your child's teacher so they something to give your child anytime they haven't been able to verify the safety of treats brought in. Parents are welcome to copy and share the cupcake recipes in this cookbook with others at their child's school as long as the title is listed as the source.

Catered events: If know in advance an event will be catered, contact the company that is catering and request an egg-free meal, or ask for a list of which foods will be safe for you to eat. They are usually happy to provide a substitute or inform you of your options as long as they are given a day or two advanced notice. If this is not possible, eating a little before you arrive, or bringing a protein bar in case it is hard to determine what is safe, can help you focus on enjoying the event regardless of what is served.

Buffet Lines: Beware! Food can be dropped from one container into nearby containers when customers are serving themselves. Look at salad bars and you will often see specks of chopped egg in the containers right next to the one with the eggs. Serving spoons can also get switched by customers from one container to another. If you are very sensitive to eggs, be careful about which foods are surrounding the food you plan to choose. The positive thing about buffets is that when there is a large selection of items to choose from, it makes it relatively easy to find something made without eggs to eat.

Leftovers: One way to adapt to having to cook frequently due to a food intolerance, is to make double batches whenever possible and freeze the leftovers in single-serve containers. That way something is ready to go on busy days. It takes very little extra time to double the recipe and get twice the results.

Suspect Foods: If you can't verify what is in foods being served at an event and you want to risk guessing, remember to always avoid these: anything with a white creamy sauce (coleslaw, veggie dip, Alfredo), anything breaded (mozzarella sticks, onion rings, tenderloins), baked goods (cookies, cake, muffins, breads-except for regular sliced sandwich bread which is usually safe), and thick desserts (cream pies, cheesecake). The more you familiarize yourself with recipes and products, the easier it will be to know what typically contains eggs. There is almost always something a person with an egg sensitivity can eat at any given event or restaurant. Learn what foods usually don't contain eggs, confirm that it is OK, and enjoy your meals out!

Ingredients and Instructions

How to Use this Cookbook

Abbreviations:

c = cup

tbsp = tablespoon

tsp = teaspoon

oz = ounces

Grouped Ingredients: The ingredients in each recipe are grouped together in paragraphs. This shows what ingredients should be mixed together during each step of the recipe. This makes the recipe easier to follow and faster to prepare.

When the instructions state to combine the 1st group of ingredients, it means mix all the ingredients in the 1st paragraph of single spaced ingredients. The paragraphs are separated by a double space. Sometimes a "group" used in the next step may contain just 1 ingredient. See below.

Example

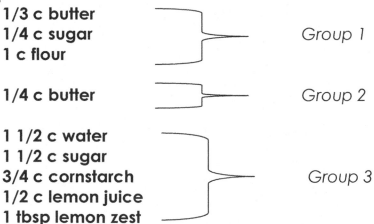

1/3 c butter
1/4 c sugar
1 c flour
Group 1

1/4 c butter
Group 2

1 1/2 c water
1 1/2 c sugar
3/4 c cornstarch
1/2 c lemon juice
1 tbsp lemon zest
Group 3

Cooking times may vary.
Your oven may require a few minutes more or less than listed. A meat thermometer should be used to verify foods reach a safe internal temperature.

What must be considered when substituting eggs?

Eggs serve multiple purposes in recipes, so the purpose they fulfill in each recipe must be considered when they are replaced. Since eggs do not fulfill the same purpose in every recipe, *there is not just one way or product that can replace eggs in everything.* This is why modifying each recipe separately is the only way to replace eggs effectively.

For example, the purpose eggs fulfill in pancakes (binding, leavening) is entirely different than what they do in mayo or French silk pie (create creaminess and volume).

Eggs can provide the following properties:

Volume

Moisture

Binding

Coating

Thickening

Leavening

Color

Creaminess

Flavor (sodium)

Emulsification

Whipping Structure

Shine

Additional Substitutions

If you are dealing with more than one food allergy, the good news is it is much easier to make one substitution than two. By starting with the recipes from this book, you are already much closer to a recipe that is suitable for you.

Suggestions for additional substitutions:

Dairy: Margarine or coconut oil for butter; rice, almond, coconut or soy milk; commercially prepared dairy-free cheese, yogurt, and cream cheese. (70% of these recipes are dairy-free or can be by substituting just butter &/or milk.)

Corn: Arrowroot powder instead of cornstarch, bread crumbs or crisp rice cereal instead of corn flakes, barley ground to the consistency of corn meal.

Nuts: SunButter® instead of peanut butter, crushed pretzels instead of chopped nuts.

Wheat or Gluten: Gluten-free flours and baking mixes, cornmeal, cornstarch, rice flour, tapioca starch, sorghum flour, potato starch. (Wheat and gluten-free substitutions have not been tested for use with these recipes. Results may vary.)

Protein Supplements: Since replacing eggs with other ingredients often does not replace the same amount of protein in a recipe, you may consider adding more protein to your diet at other times. Protein powder is a great addition to smoothies. Many varieties exist, but unflavored whey protein powder does not contain any artificial ingredients and it mixes easily. If you avoid dairy or are vegan, pea protein also is a quality protein source, although it has a stronger flavor and texture. Both are available from www.vitacost.com if you cannot find them locally.

Do you need a cookbook for additional food allergies? Visit Facebook.com/EggFreeCookbook to share your story and talk about your results after making additional substitutions, or email the author at littlethingsbooks@gmail.com.

Breakfast

Pancakes

Quick and simple.

2 c flour
1 tbsp sugar
1 tbsp baking powder
2 tsp cornstarch
1/2 tsp salt

2 c milk
1/4 c oil

butter or oil for frying

1. Combine the dry ingredients in a bowl.

2. Mix the milk and oil. Add to the flour mixture all at once. Stir with a whisk until combined and smooth.

3. Heat a frying pan on medium heat. Grease well.

4. Pour enough batter into the pan to make several 4-5" circles.

5. Fry for a few minutes until the edges look dry and bubbles appear in the center. Flip with a spatula. Grease the pan when turning over if necessary. Cook for a minute or two on the second side.

6. Repeat until all the batter has been used. Serve immediately for the best flavor and texture.

Waffles

There are a few brands of frozen waffles available in health food stores that do not contain eggs. They are usually advertised as gluten-free. But check the ingredients carefully; many gluten-free products (including waffles) do contain eggs. Some "just add water" pancake mixes also do not contain eggs and will work for making waffles at home.

1 3/4 c flour
2 tbsp cornstarch
1 tbsp sugar
1 tsp baking soda (not powder)
1/2 tsp salt

1 1/2 c milk
1/3 c oil

1. Preheat a waffle iron.

2. Combine the 1st group of ingredients. Add the milk and oil all at once and stir until smooth. Stirring with a whisk works fastest.

3. Grease the iron. Pour batter over the iron until each section is almost full.*

4. Bake for a few minutes (according to manufacturers directions) or until the amount of steam coming out of the sides has almost stopped. It may take a minute or two longer than egg-based recipes.

5. Remove with a heat-safe plastic utensil.

6. Serve immediately. If freezing for later use, cool completely before freezing.

*Check the manufacturer's instructions for your waffle iron to see how much batter is called for. Since this batter is slightly different than traditional egg-based recipes, the amount required may be a little different than what it calls for.

French Toast

This is another recipe that most people with an egg allergy have given up on completely. But it is still possible to have French toast. Try this recipe and find out for yourself!

3-4 slices of bread

1/2 c milk
3 tbsp cornstarch
1 tsp sugar
1/2 tsp vanilla
1/4 tsp cinnamon
1/8 tsp salt
1 drop yellow food coloring or a dash of turmeric spice (optional)

butter for frying

1. Toast the bread in a toaster. Do not butter. Begin heating a frying pan on medium low. Combine the 2nd group of ingredients.

2. Dip one side of the toast in the liquid mixture and quickly remove it. Dip the other side. Repeat (each side should be lightly dipped twice). The goal is to moisten the toast through to the center without completely saturating it.

3. Melt a little butter in the frying pan. Fry each side a few minutes until golden brown, adding more butter when flipping over. (If you are used to cooking French toast with eggs, this version may need to cook a bit longer on lower heat than what you are used to.)

Remember, if you are preparing regular egg-based French toast at the same time as this recipe, use separate pans, spatulas and serving dishes. Even a few crumbs from the egg-based version can cause an adverse reaction for people with an egg allergy.

Crepes

These thin and pliable French pancakes are traditionally filled with some type of filling such as fruit, rolled up, and drizzled with a sauce before serving. They are served for breakfast, but are also used in desserts and topped with whipped cream.

1 c milk
3/4 c flour*
1/4 tsp salt
1/4 tsp baking soda (not powder)
dash ground turmeric (optional for color)

butter or oil for frying

1. Combine the 1st group of ingredients. The fastest method is to use a blender.

2. Heat a non-stick frying pan on medium or an electric frying pan on 300°. A pan with very low sides works best. Grease well with butter.

3. Fill a 1/4 c measuring cup with batter. Hold the pan by the handle in 1 hand. With the other hand, poor the batter in the center of the pan. While pouring, tilt the pan to swirl the batter until it spreads out into a 7" wide circle.

4. Fry for a few minutes until the edges look cooked and bubbles appear in the center. Flip with the spatula, greasing between flips if necessary. Cook 1-2 minutes on the other side.

5. Place on a plate and cover with a towel to keep warm. Repeat until all batter has been used. Fill with desired filling and roll up.

*For dessert crepes, reduce the flour by 2 tbsp and add 2 tbsp sugar.

Makes 4-5 crepes.

Egg Patty for Breakfast Sandwich

Drive-through restaurants serve a variety of hot sandwiches with a round egg patty in between an English muffin, bagel or croissant. This is a great quick fix for a morning commute.

1/4 c water
2 tbsp cornmeal
2 tbsp shredded cheddar, mozzarella or Colby jack cheese
1 tsp cornstarch
1/4 tsp prepared yellow mustard
pinch salt

1. Butter a 3-4" wide (at the bottom) microwave safe bowl or liquid measuring cup.

2. Add the ingredients and mix everything together.

3. Microwave for 1 minute.

4. Allow to cool slightly, then run a knife around the outside edge to remove.

5. Add between 2 slices of an English muffin, bagel, croissant or toast.

6. Add cheese, sausage, ham or bacon or any other fillings desired.

My husband's favorite breakfast sandwich is made with a few slices of avocado or a generous amount of guacamole.

Omelet

This is a flavorful, though not perfect, replica of an egg omelet. It certainly expands the menu for someone looking for a savory, yet egg-free, hot breakfast.

2/3 c water
1/4 c cornmeal
1/8 tsp salt

4 tbsp parmesan

2 tbsp water
2 tbsp cornstarch

onions, peppers, spinach and/or mushrooms, etc.
sausage, bacon, or ham (optional)
shredded cheese

1. Begin heating a non-stick frying pan on medium or electric skillet on 300°.

2. Sauté the vegetables and/or meat desired for the filling. Keep warm.

3. Mix the first group of ingredients together in a microwave safe dish. Microwave for 1 minute. Stir until smooth.

4. Add the parmesan and stir in. Butter the hot frying pan well.

5. Mix the water and cornstarch together in a small dish. Add to the cornmeal mixture, stir it in, and immediately scoop the mixture into the pan. Using a heat safe spatula, flatten the mix to make a circle about 7" in diameter. Lightly pat the sides of the circle using the spatula to make them smooth.

6. Add the hot vegetable and/or meat filling and shredded cheese to one side of the omelet.

7. After the omelet has cooked about 5-7 minutes and is just beginning to brown on the bottom, flip the empty side up over the half with the filling.

8. Slide onto plate. Sprinkle the top with cheese and extra filling if desired.

Scrambled Eggs (Egg-free)

No, this is not a joke. This is a recipe for a breakfast scramble without any eggs or egg products. It's not a perfect match to scrambled eggs, but it looks similar and is easy to make. This substitution can be eaten on it's own, but it is most useful for replacing scrambled eggs in foods like breakfast burritos and breakfast pizza.

3/4 c milk
1/4 c cornmeal
3 tbsp parmesan
1 tbsp butter
1 tbsp cornstarch
1/4 tsp salt

1. Combine the ingredients in a microwave safe measuring cup or bowl.

2. Microwave for 1 1/2 minutes. Stir well.

3. Heat a skillet over medium heat. Butter the pan.

4. Pour the mixture into the pan. It will be thick. Using a heat-safe spatula, flatten the mixture into a 1/2" - 1" thick circle.

5. Stir and chop the mixture occasionally as it cooks to break it up into 1/2" - 1 1/2" pieces. Fry for 3-5 minutes until it begins to brown slightly at the edges.

Vegans often make a "scramble" from tofu because of it's high protein content. I tried working with tofu for this recipe and was not completely pleased with the results. However, if you want to use tofu, my best advise is to mash it completely with your hands and use lots of strong seasonings like onion powder and prepared mustard. Mashing the tofu makes it easier to season it thru without leaving bland centers. Topping with cheese, if possible for your diet, and/or adding salsa also helps to add flavor.

Quiche

Quiche is not just for tea rooms and fancy brunches. It's a dish that can easily be made at home to add some variety to your everyday fare.

1 - 15 oz container ricotta cheese
4 tbsp cornstarch
1 tbsp dried minced onion
3/4 tsp garlic salt
2 tsp prepared yellow mustard

10 oz frozen chopped spinach or 1 1/4 c finely chopped broccoli
1 c shredded cheddar cheese
1/2 c ham, sausage, or bacon (optional)

1 - 9" unbaked pie crust

1. Thaw the spinach or broccoli by leaving it in the refrigerator overnight, setting it out on the counter for a few hours, or defrosting it in the microwave.

2. Preheat the oven to 350°.

3. In a bowl, mix the 1st group of ingredients together.

4. Drain the broccoli or spinach (squeeze the spinach by taking one handful of spinach at a time in your hand and making a fist). Add to the mixture and stir until well combined. Fold in the shredded cheese and meat.

5. Spoon the filing into the pie crust, smoothing out the top and making it flat.

6. Bake for 45 minutes until a knife inserted in the center comes out clean.

7. Cool for a few minutes before cutting and serving.

Breakfast Casserole

This breakfast casserole is just like the strata my mother used to make for company, except the 8 eggs have been magically replaced with almost no affect on the color, texture or flavor. If you make this dish for a guest with an egg allergy, you may have to show them the recipe to prove this classic egg and cheese dish doesn't contain any eggs!

12 slices of sandwich bread

4 c milk
5 tbsp cornstarch
2 tbsp prepared yellow mustard
1 tsp garlic salt
1/4 tsp black pepper
dash of cayenne pepper

1 lb sausage, ham or bacon
1/2 a small red or yellow onion
2 stalks celery or 1 green pepper
12 oz shredded Colby jack or cheddar cheese

1. Cut the bread into small cubes. Allow it to sit out until dry, or bake it on a cookie sheet for about 20 minutes while the oven preheats to 350°.

2. Mix the 2nd group of ingredients together. Cook the meat if raw and cut it into bite size pieces. Dice the onion and celery or green pepper.

3. Grease a 9 x 13 casserole dish. Add the dry bread cubes and slowly pour the liquid mixture over the top trying to equally distribute the liquid to cover all the bread cubes.

4. Sprinkle the 3rd group of ingredients over the bread mixture, reserving a few ounces of cheese. Gently fold in the ingredients. Sprinkle the top with the remaining cheese.

5. Bake uncovered on the lower rack for 45 minutes.

This can be assembled the night before as long as it is covered and refrigerated. In the morning, remove the pan from the fridge and set it on top of the stove while the oven preheats. Cover the dish with aluminum foil and increase the baking time to 60 minutes. Test the center by inserting a knife to make sure it has set up. Bake longer if necessary.

Serves 8-10. For a smaller crowd, cut the recipe in half and bake in an 8 x 8" or a 2 Qt. casserole dish.

Breakfast Pizza

If you've never had breakfast pizza, you have been missing out!

1 pizza crust

white pizza sauce (page 99)

Egg-free scrambled eggs (page 40)

onions, green peppers and/or mushrooms
sausage, ham or bacon (optional)
shredded cheese (white or yellow)

1. Preheat the oven to 400°.
2. Prepare the crust if using a box mix or making one from scratch. Do not bake before adding the toppings.
3. Make the white sauce (page 99) and egg-free scrambled eggs (page 40). Cook the meat if raw. Cut into bite size pieces.
4. Spread the white sauce on the crust.
5. Sprinkle on the "eggs" and selected toppings.
6. Cover generously with cheese.
7. Bake for 25 minutes, or according to the instructions for the crust.

Oatmeal Supreme (Breakfast Alternative)

Although this cookbook is comprised of recipes that normally contain eggs, this recipe is included as an important exception. It helps to round out the selection for breakfast and it is so much better than traditional oatmeal. Even if you haven't cared for oatmeal in the past, give this a try. The extra ingredients turn it into a treat.

2 c water
1/4 c raisins or dried cranberries
3 tbsp brown sugar
1/2 tsp apple or pumpkin pie spice
1/2 tsp salt

1 c old-fashioned or quick rolled oats

1/2 tbsp butter or coconut oil
1/2 tsp almond extract
maple syrup or honey (optional)
milk or cream (optional)
chopped pecans or walnuts (optional)
blueberries, strawberries &/or sliced bananas (optional)

1. Pour the water into a large saucepan and place over medium high heat. Add the 1st group of ingredients to the water while it is heating.

2. Once the water begins to simmer, stir in the oats. Cover and reduce the heat to medium low. Cook for 5 minutes (quick oats) or 10 minutes for old-fashioned oats.

3. Remove from heat. Stir in the butter and almond flavor.

4. If desired, sprinkle each serving with nuts and drizzle with maple syrup and cream just before serving.

Makes 4 servings. It keeps for several days in the fridge. Microwave to reheat. Health tip: Stevia (herbal sweetener) can be used in place of brown sugar.

Apple Turnovers

Flaking and crisp with a sweet and tart filling. These look beautiful on a plate of pastries. Try making several of the recipes on the following pages when using puff pastry. It is easy to create individual treats with great variety with little time invested.

frozen puff pastry

1 apple (per 2 turnovers)
2 tsp sugar (per apple)
dash cinnamon

1 tbsp honey
1 tbsp water
sugar

1. Remove the amount of puff pastry desired from the freezer. Thaw according to package directions. A 17.3 oz box will make 8 turnovers.

2. Preheat the oven to 400°. Peel and dice the apple(s). Sprinkle with the cinnamon and sugar. Microwave 2 minutes per apple. Dice the cooked apple slices.

3. Unfold each sheet of pastry and cut in half in both directions to make 4 - 5x5" squares.

4. Place on an ungreased cookie sheet. Add 2 tbsp of the apple filling to one side of each turnover (imagine a diagonal folding line from one corner to the other).

5. Mix the honey and water. Brush the edges of the dough. Fold diagonally to make a triangle, pressing with fingers into the dough to seal the edges.

6. Brush the tops of the turnovers with the honey mixture. (This adds brown color and a slight gloss, which is typically achieved in bakeries with an egg wash.) Sprinkle with sugar.

7. Bake for 20 minutes. Cool a few minutes before serving.

Raspberry Danish

It's so hard to pass by a window of delicious pastries at a bakery, knowing you probably can't have any of them. But with the following recipes, you now have an easy way to create many varieties of delectable flaky pastries!

1 box frozen puff pastry
1 heaping tbsp raspberry* preserves per Danish

1 tsp honey
1 tsp water

1. Remove only the amount of pastry desired from the freezer and thaw according to package directions. A 17.3 oz box has enough to make 8 Danishes. To make just 2, thaw only 1/2 of a roll.

2. Preheat oven to 400°.

3. Unfold the pastry (into a 10"x10" square). Cut the pastry in half going both directions to make 5x5" squares.

4. Place each square on an ungreased cookie sheet.

5. Roll the edges in about 1", pressing down lightly with a finger every 1/2" to seal. This will make a ring around the outside edge of the pastry.

6. Mix the honey and water and brush around outside ring. This adds brown color and a slight gloss, which is typically achieved with an egg wash.

7. Bake for 10 minutes.

8. Remove from the oven and spread a heaping tablespoon of preserves in the center of each pastry.

9. Bake for an additional 10 minutes. Allow to cool a few minutes before serving. Drizzle with icing if desired.

*Any type of jelly or preserves can be used. Cream cheese can also be added.

Donuts

If you have never considered making donuts before, take a crack at it- without cracking any eggs. If you don't have a donut cutter (they can be hard to find), cut both ends off of a tomato paste can. Clean well and use it to cut the 2" center hole after cutting the large circle with a biscuit cutter or a 4" wide drinking glass. Or, skip cutting the dough altogether by rolling the entire batch into 1 1/4" wide donut holes with your hands.

2 c flour
1/2 c sugar
1 tbsp baking powder
1/2 tsp nutmeg
1/4 tsp salt

3/4 c milk
2 tbsp melted butter

1. Combine the dry ingredients in a large bowl. Melt the butter and add to the dry ingredients along with the milk. Stir until combined.

2. Turn onto a floured work surface. Knead slightly (less than 1 minute) just to pull the dough together. When it is well combined and slightly stretchy it is ready.

3. Heat 3" of oil in a deep fryer, an electric frying pan or a small saucepan on the stovetop to 350°. For best results on the stove top, use a thermometer for accuracy.

4. Roll out to 1/4" thickness. Cut out donut shapes. Roll the scrap pieces into 1" balls to make additional donut holes. (Fry about 1 minute until brown on the bottom, then flip over to fry an additional minute. Carefully remove from the oil and dry on paper towels.

5. After cooling for a few minutes, roll in cinnamon sugar, or in a glaze made from mixing 1/2 c powdered sugar with 2 tbsp milk and a dash of salt.

Makes 6 donuts and 12 donut holes.

Baked Goods

Blueberry Muffins

Large bakery style muffins, with a crisp sugary top. Frozen blueberries bake as well as fresh, but are readily available all year, easy to keep on hand and more economical.

1 1/2 c flour
3/4 c frozen blueberries
3/4 c sugar
2 tbsp cornstarch
3/4 tsp baking soda (not powder)
3/4 tsp salt

2/3 c milk
1/3 c oil

2 tbsp sugar
1/8 tsp cinnamon

1. Preheat the oven to 400°. Grease 6 regular sized muffin tins or insert paper liners.

2. Mix together the 1st group of ingredients. Do not thaw the blueberries. Simply add them to the flour mixture frozen.

3. Measure the milk and oil together in a liquid measuring cup. Pour over the flour mixture all at once. Stir gently just until combined.

4. Fill prepared muffin cups *to the top* with batter. This will create a large muffin top like those purchased in bakeries.

5. Combine the cinnamon and sugar. Sprinkle the top of the batter in each muffin cup generously.

6. Bake for 30 minutes. Allow to cool for several minutes before removing them from the tin.

Makes 6 large bakery style muffins.

Bran Muffins

Classic bran muffins.

4 c bran cereal flakes
1 1/2 c milk
1/2 c mashed banana (1 medium)
2 tbsp oil

1 c flour
1/2 c brown sugar
1 tbsp baking powder
1 tsp cinnamon

1. Preheat the oven to 350°.
2. Pour the bran flakes in a large mixing bowl and cover with the milk. Let sit for 5 minutes to soften the cereal.
3. Mash the banana and add to the cereal along with the oil. Grease 12 muffin tin spaces or line with paper lines.
4. In a separate bowl mix the dry ingredients together. Add the moistened cereal and mix lightly until combined.
5. Fill each space in the muffin pan almost to the top with batter.
6. Bake for 30 minutes. Allow to cool before serving.

Makes 12 muffins.

Cinnamon Rolls

Ready-to-bake cinnamon rolls can be purchased in the frozen food section of your grocery store. Many contain eggs as do traditional recipes from scratch, but it is common to find brands that do not.

1 packet rapid rise yeast
3 tbsp lukewarm water
1/2 tsp honey

3/4 c milk
3 tbsp honey
3 tbsp melted butter

2 3/4 c flour
1/4 c instant mashed potato flakes
1/2 tsp salt

1/2 c sugar
2 tbsp butter
2 tsp cinnamon

1. In a small bowl or mug, mix the first 3 ingredients and allow to stand while mixing the other ingredients-at least 5 minutes or until foamy.

2. Melt the butter. Mix with the milk and honey. They mixture should be slightly warm.

3. Mix the dry ingredients in a large bowl. Add the yeast mixture and the liquid ingredients and stir until combined.

4. Knead 5-7 minutes. Place the dough into an greased bowl and cover. Allow to rise for 1 hour, or until double in size.

5. Melt the butter and mix the cinnamon and sugar.

6. Roll the dough out into a 12" x 12" rectangle.

7. Brush the melted butter over the dough. Sprinkle all of the sugar mixture over the dough.

8. Roll up the dough. Cut into 12—1" pieces. Place the cinnamon rolls flat side down in two greased 9" round pans or pie plates.

9. Cover and let rise for 1 hour or until double in size.

10. Preheat the oven to 350°. Bake for 18 minutes or until the tops are brown. Cool slightly and remove from pan.

11. Allow to cool slightly and brush the tops with butter or spread a thin layer of icing. To make icing, mix 1/2 cup powdered sugar with 2 teaspoons of milk and a dash of salt.

Sticky rolls

To make sticky rolls, mix the following while the dough is rising: 1/3 c brown sugar, 2 tbsp butter, and 1 tbsp corn syrup. Cook over low heat in a saucepan until melted and combined. Pour into the bottom of the pan before adding the rolls. Pecans can also be added if desired.

Tips:

Instant mashed potatoes come in the form of flakes or granules. Either can be used. Granules will make the dough look lumpy during kneading and rising, but the rolls will turn out fine.

The oven is a great place to allow dough to rise. Leave the oven off but turn the light on. The light bulb will warm the oven.

Coffee Cake

Wonderful crumb texture with a simple fruit ribbon and streusel topping.

1 3/4 c flour
3/4 c sugar
1/2 tsp baking powder
3/4 tsp baking soda
1/4 tsp salt

2/3 c milk
1/3 c oil
1 tbsp lemon juice

1/2 c jam or preserves (optional)

Topping:
1/4 c (2 oz) chopped pecans or walnuts (optional)
1/4 c brown sugar
1/4 tsp cinnamon

1. Preheat oven to 350°. Grease an 8 x 8 pan.

2. Combine the 1st group of ingredients in a large bowl and mix well. A whisk works quickly.

3. Measure the milk, oil, and lemon juice together in a measuring cup. Add to the dry ingredients all at once. Stir just until combined.

4. Spread 2/3rds of the batter in the bottom of the pan. Drop the jam over the batter by teaspoonfuls. Drop the remaining batter over the top by spoonfuls. Do not spread out. This will create a wonderful varied texture to the top.

5. Combine the brown sugar, nuts, and cinnamon. Sprinkle over the top. Do not pat down.

6. Bake for 35 minutes.

Scones

These triangular shaped coffee house treats make a great breakfast to go. They have a crisp crust and tender crumbly interior texture.

3 c flour
3/4 c sugar
2 tbsp cornstarch
1 tsp baking soda (not powder)
1/2 tsp salt

1/2 c butter
1/2 c dried cranberries or raisins

1/2 c + 2 tbsp milk
2 tbsp lemon juice

1. Preheat oven to 400°

2. Mix the 1st group of ingredients in a bowl. Cut in the butter with a pastry cutter or fork until it is the size of small peas. Stir in the cranberries or raisins.

3. Mix together the milk and lemon juice. Slowly drizzle over the dry ingredients, stopping to stir a few times before it has all been added. The mixture will be very crumbly and dry.

4. Turn out onto a clean countertop. Gently pull the dough together with your hands, pressing down on it and turning it a few times until it comes together to form a ball. It will seem like there is not enough liquid at first, but in about 1 minute it should form a nice dough. If it still doesn't, drizzle 1 tsp of milk at a time over the loose flour, mixing again after each addition until it does.

5. Pat the dough into a flat-topped 8 inch circle. Sprinkle with sugar.

6. Make 4 cuts across the dough to make 8 pieces (like cutting a pizza). Place each triangle shaped scone on a lightly greased cookie sheet.

7. Bake 20 minutes. Cool on a wire rack.

Banana Bread

Moist with plenty of banana flavor.

2 c mashed bananas (5-6 medium bananas)
1 1/2 c sugar
1/2 c butter

3 c flour
2 tsp baking soda (not powder)
1/2 tsp salt

1/2 c chopped nuts (optional)

1. Preheat oven to 350°

2. Mash bananas with a fork or an electric mixer. Cream with the sugar and butter.

3. Combine the flour, baking soda, and salt in a separate bowl. Add to the banana mixture and mix just until combined.

4. Grease the bottom and corners (but not the sides) of 2 bread pans. Pour the batter into the pans and bake on the middle rack for 60 minutes.

Cool for 10 minutes on a wire rack. Loosen the edges with a knife. Remove the loaves and finish cooling on the wire rack.

Makes 2 loaves.

Pumpkin Bread

Sugar and spice and everything nice. Makes a great treat to wrap up and give away.

2 c flour
2 1/2 tsp pumpkin pie spice
2 tsp baking powder
1/2 tsp baking soda
3/4 tsp salt

1 c canned pumpkin
1 cup brown sugar
3/4 c water
1/2 c oil

1. Preheat the oven to 350°. Grease a loaf pan.

2. Mix together the 1st group of ingredients in a large bowl.

3. Stir together the 2nd group of ingredients in a measuring cup or bowl. Stir until all sugar lumps are broken up.

4. Add to the dry ingredients. Stir just until combined.

5. Pour into the pan. Bake for 50 minutes or until a toothpick inserted in the center comes out clean.

6. Cool on a wire rack. Cool at least 10 minutes before removing from pan.

Pumpkin Muffins: Fill 18 muffin tins with paper liners. Fill with the batter (about 3/4 full). Bake 20 minutes.

Optional ingredients to add: chopped walnuts, pecans, chocolate chips or raisins.

Corn Bread

There is no risk that this corn bread will turn out dry. This recipe is a good balance between Southern-style and sweet varieties that is full of flavor.

1 c cornmeal
1 1/2 c milk
1/4 c oil

1 c flour
1/4 c sugar
2 tbsp cornstarch
1 1/2 tbsp baking powder
1 1/2 tsp salt

1. Preheat oven to 400°

2. Mix the cornmeal, milk and oil. Allow to soak while mixing the other ingredients. This makes the cornbread extra moist.

3. In a separate bowl, mix the second group of ingredients. Add to the cornmeal mix. Stir until just a few lumps remain.

4. Pour into a greased 8 x 8 pan or a round 9" pan and bake 35 minutes.

    - or -

    Pour into greased muffin tins and bake 12 minutes (makes 18 muffins).

    - or -

    For large crowds, make a double batch and pour into a greased 16 x 12 x 1 cookie sheet and bake 20 minutes.

Test to see if it is done by inserting a toothpick into the center. If it comes out clean it is done.

Oatmeal Dinner Rolls

These filling rolls make a pan large enough to feed a crowd. They are simple to make for a yeast bread and the perfect compliment to soups and stews.

4 c milk
1 packet dry yeast

7 c flour
2 c quick oats
1/4 c sugar
2 tsp salt
1 tsp baking soda (not powder)
1/3 c oil

1. Warm the milk to just above skin temperature (110°). Stir in the yeast. Let sit for 5 minutes until frothy.

2. Turn the light in the oven on, but leave the oven off. The light bulb will warm the oven slightly, making it a great place for the rolls to rise.

3. Mix the remaining ingredients together in a large bowl. Add the milk and yeast and stir until combined.

4. Grease a cookie sheet. Spread the dough over the cookie sheet. Cover with a clean towel and let rise in the warm oven for 1 hour.

5. Remove the dough from the oven. Preheat oven to 350°.

6. Cut the dough in the pan into dinner roll sized pieces (3-5") using a butter knife. If the dough is very soft, wet the knife with water to assist in scoring the dough.

7. Bake for 15 minutes or until the tops begin to brown slightly.

Try serving these rolls warm with honey butter.

Dinner Rolls

Few breads compare to the sweet taste and tender texture of these glorious homemade rolls. A few varieties of frozen dinner rolls come egg-free. But these fresh rolls are well worth the extra hands-on time required to prepare.

1 packet rapid rise yeast
3 tbsp lukewarm water
1/2 tsp honey

3/4 c milk
3 tbsp melted butter
3 tbsp honey

2 3/4 c flour
1/4 c instant mashed potato flakes
1/2 tsp salt

1. In a small bowl or mug, mix the yeast with tap water that is just slightly warm to the touch, along with a small squeeze of honey to feed the yeast.

2. Melt the butter and mix with the milk and honey in a separate bowl. (The mixture should be slightly warm.)

3. Mix the dry ingredients together in a large bowl.

4. Once the yeast looks foamy (5-10 minutes), add it to the flour along with the other liquid ingredients. Stir until combined. Turn out onto a work surface. Knead 5-7 minutes until the dough feels slightly firm and stretchy.

5. Place the dough in an oiled bowl and cover. Allow to rise in a warm place* until double in size-about 1 hour.

6. Grease a cookie sheet. Divide the dough into 12 equal pieces. Roll into balls and pull the dough together at the bottom, pinching the dough to keep it together . Cover and allow to rise until double– about 1 hour.

7. Brush with melted butter, or "egg wash" (p 64).

8. Bake at 350° for 15 minutes.

Cloverleaf rolls: Divide the dough into 36 pieces. Oil a muffin tin. Roll the dough into balls and place 3 balls in every muffin tin space to create 12 cloverleaf rolls.

Whole Wheat: Replace up to half of the flour with whole wheat flour. Increase the salt to 3/4 tsp. Knead for 7-8 minutes.

Tips

*The oven is a great place to allow dough to rise. Turn the light inside the oven on, but leave the oven itself off. The light bulb will help to warm it slightly.

Instant mashed potatoes come in the form of flakes or granules. Either can be used. Granules will make the dough look lumpy during kneading and rising, but the rolls will turn out fine.

An "egg" wash can be added before baking to make the rolls brown. Simply mix 1 Tbsp honey with 1 Tbsp water. (See details on page 64.) Or, the tops of the rolls can be buttered after coming out of the oven to give them added shine.

Egg Wash for Baked Goods

Egg washes are used to help baked goods brown and develop a slight sheen. They can often knock out an entire bakery's selection for someone with an egg allergy. *If you have favorite bread recipes or other items that do not contain eggs except for the egg wash, simply use this recipe to keep your old recipes safe for everyone at the table.*

1 tbsp honey
1 tbsp water

1. Stir until honey is mixed completely with the water.

2. Brush on baked goods with a pastry brush before baking.

If you want to add extra shine, after the "egg washed" baked goods come out of the oven, rub the top with a small amount of butter.

Bread Bear

This is one of the cutest baked goods you can make. It makes a great get well, welcome to the neighborhood, or new baby gift.

1. Using the Dinner Roll recipe on page 62 (or 12 frozen dinner rolls), shape into a teddy bear after the 1st rise (or after thawing the rolls for 1 hour).

2. Grease a cookie sheet, or if you want to give it away without having to collect your pan later, cover a piece of cardboard with heavy duty aluminum foil.

3. Cut the dough in half and use one half to shape the body (or knead 5 rolls together). Shape into an oval and flatten slightly. Place on the cookie sheet a little below the center of the pan.

4. Divide the remaining dough in half. Work one of the halves (or knead together 2 1/2 rolls) into a circle, flatten slightly and place a little above the body to create the head.

5. Remove about 1/4 of the remaining dough (or 1/2 a roll), and roll into 3 balls. Flatten two slightly and place at the top of the head for ears. Flatten the 3rd to 1/2 the width of the head, and place at the bottom of the head for a muzzle.

6. Divide the remaining dough into 4 pieces (or use 4 rolls). Roll into short cylinders, placing at the bears side's for arms and legs.

7. Cut slits in the dough for eyes, nose and a belly button and insert raisins. Brush with melted butter or "egg" wash (page 64). Cover with a clean towel and place someplace warm. Let rise 1 hour or until about double in size. Bake at 350° for 20 minutes.

8. After the bear has cooled, cut a piece of ribbon used for wrapping gifts, tie into a bow and press the knot into the crease of the neck using the tip of a pointy knife.

Salads, Dressings, & Dips

Mayonnaise

Egg-free (vegan) mayonnaise is sold at health food stores, but it can be hard to find and expensive. This is a simple alternative. It will not keep for weeks in the fridge like a jar of commercial mayonnaise with preservatives. But it is easy to mix together and offers an authentic flavor that can't be matched.

1/2 c milk
1 1/2 tbsp cornstarch

1 tbsp lemon juice
1/4 tsp salt

1/2 c oil

1. Whisk together the milk and cornstarch in a small saucepan. Place over medium-high heat on the stovetop. Stir with a whisk until thick and bubbly, about 2 minutes.

2. Remove from heat. Add the lemon juice and salt.

3. Slowly add the oil in a thin stream while whisking. If the oil starts to separate from the mayonnaise at any time, stop pouring and whisk until blended before adding more oil. If the oil is added too fast, it may separate and ruin the batch.

Store in the refrigerator. Remember to keep any dishes made with this mayonnaise in the refrigerator or on ice (such as at picnics) as it contains dairy. This mayonnaise is designed to be thick, but spreadable, when cold.

* It takes less than 5 minutes to whisk this recipe by hand, but an immersion blender (stick blender) can be used. Place the mixture in a narrow jar and use an up and down motion while the oil is added. A regular blender can be used, but it is messier and the sides must be scrapped frequently.

Veggie Dip

Vegetable dip found in the produce isle usually contains eggs, along with heavy amounts of oil. Not only is this dip egg-free, it is considerably lower in fat and calories and contains beneficial probiotics and calcium. A ready-made alternative is sour cream based dips found in the dairy section which are usually egg-free as well. The main lesson to learn about vegetable dips is to never that they are egg-free without checking the label.

1 - 6 oz container plain yogurt (Greek or regular)
1 tsp oil
1 tsp dried dill
1/4 tsp garlic salt
1/4 tsp onion powder
dash cayenne
black pepper to taste

1. Mix well.

2. Chill to marry the flavors.

Whipped Salad Dressing

Sweet and tangy mayo style products are something people who discover they have an egg sensitivity later in life really miss. This recipe takes more effort than just grabbing a jar off the shelf. But, being able to whip up a safe version of this classic white cream at home is like a miracle if you can't have similar products from the store.

1 c milk
3 tbsp cornstarch

6 tbsp powdered sugar
6 tbsp vinegar*
1/2 tsp salt
1/8 tsp dry mustard

1 c oil

1. Whisk the milk and cornstarch together in a small saucepan. Place over medium-high heat on the stovetop. Cook and stir until thick and creamy, about 3 minutes.

2. Remove from heat. Scrape the mixture into a large glass jar such as a wide mouthed quart jar or pickle jar.

3. Add the 2nd group of ingredients.

4. Using an immersion blender (stick blender)**, blend until the ingredients are combined.

5. Measure the oil in a measuring cup that has a pouring spout if possible. Pour a tiny amount of oil (about 1 tsp) into the jar. Blend until combined. An up and down motion works best for this recipe.

6. Repeat adding oil in tiny amounts and blending between each addition, until all the oil has been used. (Adding too much at once may cause the oil to separate from the other ingredients and ruin the batch.)

Keep refrigerated. Since this does not have preservatives like commercial varieties, it is especially important to only insert clean utensils into the jar and to throw it out after a few days or immediately if any change in color or texture is observed. Keep any foods made with this salad dressing refrigerated.

This recipe makes a large jar. If you need less, a half a recipe has enough volume that it can be mixed with a stick blender.

* Use white distilled vinegar, or half white/ half apple cider vinegar to produce the best flavor.

** A regular blender can be used, but it is far messier and frequent scrapping of the sides is required to get the thick mixture to blend. If you plan to make this recipe often, an immersion blender is an inexpensive appliance that is well worth the cost.

Potato Salad

It is easy to leave the out the hardboiled eggs when making potato salad. The hard part is figuring out how to replace the mayonnaise. This recipe eliminates the need for expensive and hard to find egg-free mayonnaise, or the time required to make your own from scratch.

2 lbs potatoes (6 cups diced, about 5-6 white or 8-10 red potatoes)

8 oz sour cream
2 tbsp vinegar
1 tbsp honey
1 tbsp mustard
1 tsp salt
1 tsp dried parsley, basil, or dill
1/2 c sweet pickle relish

3 stalks celery
1/2 a red onion
bacon crumbles (optional)

1. Wash and dice the potatoes (the skins add color and flavor but can be peeled first if you prefer).

2. Boil in heavily salted water until a fork can pierce through without a hard center (10-15 minutes depending on the size of the dice).

3. Drain the potatoes into a strainer. Rinse with cold tap water for 2 minutes to reduce the temperature and stop the cooking.

4. Mix the second group of ingredients together in a large bowl. Add the potatoes and stir gently to distribute the sour cream mix.

5. Dice the celery and the onion and bacon if desired and fold them in with the potatoes.

Refrigerate until ready to serve.

Coleslaw

Allowing the cabbage to wilt makes it easy to achieve the perfect consistency-slightly softened, but with a little crunch.

1 - 14 oz bag shredded cabbage coleslaw mix
1/4 c sugar
1/2 tsp salt

1/3 c sour cream

black pepper (optional)

1. Pour the shredded cabbage into a very large bowl. Sprinkle the sugar and salt over the top and toss to distribute.

2. Place in the refrigerator, uncovered, for 15 minutes - 2 hours (longer creates a softer, less crunchy coleslaw).

3. Drain the liquid that has collected at the bottom of the bowl.

4. Add the sour cream to the cabbage and mix well until evenly distributed.

Alternate recipes: In place of the sour cream, Vidalia® Onion Dressing or honey mustard dressing make an excellent coleslaw. Some brands of these dressings are egg-free. But check carefully-many are not. **If using dressing in place or sour cream, reduce the sugar used to wilt the coleslaw to 2 tbsp and use 1/2 c dressing**.

Mayonnaise (page 68) or Whipped Salad Dressing (page 70) from this cookbook can also be used in place of sour cream.

Pasta Salad

This recipe makes a creamy-sweet pasta salad like what is served in most delis. A savory alternative is to use Italian dressing alone. It gives a great flavor, but it does tend to soak into the pasta salad in the fridge. If you plan to make this ahead of time for a potluck or sack lunch, the creamy version holds up better.

12 oz rotini spiral pasta
2 c finely diced vegetables

8 oz plain yogurt
1/2 c bottled Italian salad dressing*
1 tbsp sugar

1. Cook the pasta in heavily salted water according to package directions.

2. Mix the yogurt, dressing and sugar in a large bowl. Add the pasta and veggies along with any additional ingredients desired. Stir well.

3. Keep refrigerated.

Ideas: Vegetables: celery, red onion, red or bell pepper, baby carrots. Extra ingredients to add: diced cheese, salami, or black olives.

To speed up this recipe, use 2 - 16 oz bags of frozen pasta and vegetables. Thaw by placing in the refrigerator overnight, by setting out on counter for 2 hours, or by removing from the package and defrosting in the microwave.

*Regular and light bottled Italian dressing usually do not contain eggs, but creamy Italian may. Check the label.

Seven Layer Salad

A creamy make-ahead salad that is famous as a traditional potluck side. This cool creamy salad appeals to almost everyone-even those who don't usually like leafy green salads.

1 head romaine lettuce

2 cups plain yogurt
1 cup sour cream
1/4 c sugar

1/2 head cauliflower
2 green onions
16 oz frozen peas, thawed

1 cup cheddar cheese
1/4 c crumbled cooked bacon or bacon bits

1. Wash, dry and cut the lettuce in a large dice. Spread out in a 9 x 13 pan or place in a very large glass bowl if you would like the layers to be visible.

2. Combine the yogurt, sour cream, sugar. Pour 1/2 of the mixture over the lettuce and stir to lightly coat the lettuce.

3. Finely chop the cauliflower and layer over the lettuce. Slice the green onions and layer over the cauliflower, saving some for a garnish if desired. Spread the peas evenly over the top of the salad.

4. Pour the remaining dressing over the top and spread evenly with a spatula.

5. Cover and refrigerate several hours or overnight to blend the flavors.

6. When ready to serve, layer with the cheese, bacon and remaining green onions.

Alternate: The yogurt and sour cream can be replaced with Mayonnaise from page 68. Or, use Whipped Salad Dressing from page 70 as the dressing here.

Ranch Dressing

Bottled ranch dressing almost always contains eggs. This easy recipe makes this favorite classic dressing in almost no time at all.

1/2 c sour cream
3 tbsp milk
1/2 tsp garlic salt
1/2 tsp onion powder
1/4 tsp black pepper
1/4 tsp dried dill (optional)

1. Whisk to combine.
2. Store in the refrigerator.

Makes 2-4 servings.

Homemade dressings will not keep as long in the refrigerator as commercially prepared versions because they do not contain preservatives. Prepare only what you plan to use immediately or within a few days. I

t is easy to cut the recipe in half if less is needed. (1/2 of a tablespoon is 1 1/2 teaspoons.)

Caesar Salad Dressing

A strong flavored dressing designed to be tossed with the salad in a large bowl before serving.

1/2 c sour cream
1 tsp garlic salt
2 tsp Worcestershire sauce
1 tbsp parmesan cheese
1 tsp anchovy paste or mashed anchovy filets*

1. Combine in a bowl or small jar.
2. Toss with salad in a large bowl to distribute a small amount of dressing over the salad.

* If you do not have anchovies, add an extra 1/2 tsp of garlic salt.

Thousand Island Dressing

It is easy to recreate this dressing without eggs once you know it can be done with just four ingredients.

1/2 c sour cream
1/2 c sweet pickle relish
4 tsp ketchup
1 tsp yellow prepared mustard

1. Stir together in a small bowl.

2. Serve using a small spoon to drizzle the dressing over the salad.

Use to make a Reuben sandwich. Place hot corned beef and sauerkraut on toasted rye and add a generous amount of thousand island dressing.

Blue Cheese Dressing

It's easy to make this distinctive salad dressing at home without the eggs used in bottled dressings.

1/2 c sour cream
1 tbsp milk
1 tsp vinegar
1/2 tsp garlic salt

1/4 c blue cheese crumbles

1. Mix the 1st group of ingredients together.

2. Break up the blue cheese into tiny crumbles.

3. Stir into the dressing.

Makes 2-4 servings. It is easy to cut the recipe in half if less is needed. (1/2 of a tablespoon is 1 1/2 teaspoons.)

Honey Mustard Dressing/Dipping Sauce

A classic tangy and sweet salad dressing or dipping sauce for chicken nuggets or chicken wings, yet without the eggs and high amounts of fat in many traditional versions.

2 tbsp prepared yellow mustard
2 tbsp honey
1 tbsp oil (omit for dipping sauce)

1. Mix together in a small serving bowl, or place in a jar with a tight fitting lid and shake to combine.

Adjust the sweet/tart ratio of honey to mustard to your individual preference.

Tartar Sauce

So simple to prepare, and just as tasty as classic versions.

1/2 c sour cream
1/2 c sweet pickle relish
pinch salt
dash pepper

1. Mix together in a small serving bowl.
2. Serve.

Spinach Dip

There's nothing like a cool flavorful dip for game time or a party. It's also the tastiest way to eat one of the healthiest foods on the planet. Serve with Wheat Thins®, Pita chips, or fresh veggie sticks.

1 10 oz. package frozen chopped spinach

1 package cream cheese
2 - 6 oz containers plain yogurt
1 tsp garlic salt

1/2 a red bell pepper

1. Thaw spinach by placing in refrigerator overnight for best results. Or, set out on counter for a few hours, place the package in a plastic baggie and soak in warm water, or defrost in the microwave.

2. Using an electric mixer, mix the cream cheese, yogurt and garlic salt until smooth. A whisk or fork can be used, but it will take several minutes to achieve a smooth consistency.

3. Take one handful of spinach at a time in your hand and squeeze it into a fist to press it dry. Crumble the spinach into the cream cheese mixture and stir well to combine.

4. Dice the bell pepper and stir into the dip, saving a few to garnish the top.

Refrigerate until served. Best if served the same day.

Spinach Artichoke Dip

A hot dip like the appetizer served at many Italian restaurants. This packs a flavor punch and cuts out the egg-containing mayonnaise. Serve with toasted baguette slices, tortilla chips or warm flat bread.

10 oz package frozen chopped spinach

1 - 8 oz package cream cheese
1 - 7.5 oz jar artichoke hearts, drained (optional)
1 c shredded mozzarella or white cheddar cheese
1/4 c grated parmesan cheese
1/2 a yellow or white onion
2-3 large cloves of garlic
3/4 tsp salt
1/4 tsp cayenne pepper

1/2 c shredded mozzarella or white cheddar cheese

1. Thaw spinach (place in fridge overnight for best results, or set out on the counter for a few hours, place package in a plastic baggie and soak in warm water, or defrost in the microwave). Do not drain or squeeze dry.

2. Preheat the oven to 350°. Grease a 1.5 Qt. casserole dish.

3. Finely mince the onion press the garlic. Drain the artichoke hearts and separate the leaves.

4. Mix the spinach and 2nd group of ingredients together in a bowl. Pour into the casserole dish and spread evenly. Sprinkle the last 1/2 c of cheese over the top.

5. Bake for 30 minutes.

If using baguette slices, which are excellent with this dip, place them on a cookie sheet and toast them in the oven the last 5-10 minutes of baking time.

Main Dishes

Tuna Salad Sandwiches

Serve cold in your favorite sandwich bread or a pita pocket, or grill for a hot sandwich with melted cheese.

1 can tuna

2 tbsp sour cream
2 tbsp sweet pickle relish
1/4 tsp prepared mustard
pinch salt

1 stalk celery (optional)

1. Drain the tuna.

2. Combine the 2nd group of ingredients together in a bowl. Add the tuna and mix well.

3. Finely dice the celery and stir it into the mix.

When packing a lunch, consider keeping the filing separate from the bread in a small plastic container.

Tuna Sandwich

Mix yellow mustard - honey relish with small amount of Carnation milk - can add celery.

Chicken Salad Sandwiches

This chicken salad makes a filling lunch or an elegant party sandwich. Can be made ahead and kept in the refrigerator.

3 c mashed cooked chicken (about 3 large chicken breasts)

3/4 c sour cream
3 tbsp sugar
2 tbsp pickle relish
1 1/2 tsp prepared yellow mustard
3/4 tsp onion powder
3/4 tsp salt

1/4 c diced celery (optional)

1. Cook the chicken. Dice and then mash with your fingers or a fork, or pulse in a food processor (the food processor is easiest and produces the creamiest sandwich spread).

2. Mix together the 2nd group of ingredients in a small bowl (or add to the food processor bowl).

3. Add the chicken and celery and mix until well combined.

4. Spread between slices of bread, put in pita pockets or roll up in tortillas to make pinwheels.

Optional ingredients can be added such as finely diced onion, green onion, halved green grapes, watercress, chopped walnuts or slivered almonds.

To make finger sandwiches for a party, fill the bread, cut off the crust and make 2 diagonal cuts to make 4 small triangular sandwiches. For added variety, use 2 different kinds of bread on each side of the sandwich.

Egg Salad Sandwiches

This sandwich goes together quickly and is also rich in protein. It's easy to make a single serving for someone with an egg allergy when egg salad sandwiches are being served so they won't feel left out.

3/4 c small curd cottage cheese
2 tsp prepared yellow mustard
2 tsp sugar
1/2 tsp white vinegar
1/8 tsp onion powder (optional)
pinch salt and pepper

1 tbsp dry bread crumbs

4 slices of bread

1. Stir the 1st group of ingredients together to combine.

2. Stir in the bread crumbs and allow it to rest for 5 minutes.

3. Fill the bread slices to make 2 full sandwiches.

Additional ingredients can be added to customize such as pickle relish, or finely diced celery or onion.

Ham Salad Sandwiches

This simple recipe reproduces an old classic. It's a great spread to keep in the fridge, so sandwiches can be whipped up in a snap. It also makes elegant tea party sandwiches when the crust is cut off and each sandwich is sliced diagonally twice in order to create 4 mini triangle sandwiches.

1 pound ham
6 oz plain yogurt
1/4 c sour cream
2 Tbsp sugar

1. Dice the ham.

2. Add all the ingredients to a food processor or blender. (If using a blender do in 2 batches)

3. Process until ham is smooth.

4. Chill until ready to use.

5. Serve on bread or buns.

Pickle relish can be added if desired.

Topping + little too sweet

Meatloaf ✓

Here is another American classic that has always included eggs to hold the final product together. But eggs can also make a meatloaf tough. No one will miss them in this moist, delicious meatloaf.

1 lb lean ground beef or turkey
3/4 c dry breadcrumbs (*Check the label. Some brands contain eggs!!!*)
1/4 c milk
1/4 c ketchup
2 tsp dried minced onion
1/2 tsp garlic salt

1/4 c ketchup
3 tbsp brown sugar
1 tbsp yellow prepared mustard

1. Preheat the oven to 350°.

2. Put the ground meat in a bowl. Sprinkle the bread crumbs on top and add the extra ingredients from the first group of ingredients. Combine well (using your hands works best).

3. Press the mixture into a loaf pan and even out the top with a fork.

4. Combine the second group of ingredients. Spread over the top of the loaf.

5. Bake for 1 hour.

Variations:

Philly Cheese Steak Loaf: Add green peppers and mushrooms to the meatloaf and top with a white cheese instead of the ketchup sauce.

Steakhouse Meatloaf: Replace the ketchup with steak sauce for a sophisti-cated flavor.

Meatballs

Hearty meatballs that cook quickly on the stove top in the same pan as the spaghetti sauce.

1 lb ground beef
3/4 c dry bread crumbs
1/4 c milk
2 tsp dry minced onion
1 tsp garlic salt
1 tsp Italian seasoning

oil for frying

1. Begin heating a large heavy pot over medium heat. Add enough oil to just cover the bottom of the pan.

2. Place the ingredients in a bowl. Using your hands, mix the ingredients together well.

3. Roll the mixture into 1 1/4" balls. Place in the pan as they are made.

4. Turn each meatball over after it browns on one side. After the meatballs brown on the second side, begin turning ever 30 seconds or so until they are mostly browned on the outside (total frying time approximately 10 minutes).

5. Pour 2 jars of spaghetti sauce over the meatballs in the pot. Stir and cover. Keep heat on medium or medium low so the sauce bubbles rapidly. Allow the meatballs to cook for 15 minutes, or until no longer pink inside.

If not cooking in spaghetti sauce, continue turning and frying until cooked through, or bake in a 350° oven for approximately 45 minutes instead of frying.

Makes 16 meatballs.

Sweet n' Sour Meatballs

These sweet and sour tender meatballs are great as party appetizers or the main course for dinner.

1 lb ham
1 lb ground pork, beef or turkey
1 1/2 c graham cracker crumbs
1/2 c milk
1/4 c ketchup

1 c brown sugar
1/2 c ketchup
1/4 c prepared yellow mustard
1/4 c apple cider vinegar

1. Preheat the oven to 350°.

2. Cut the ham into a large dice and place it in a food processor. Turn on and process for a minute or two, stopping to scrape the sides as needed until it is very fine and smooth.

3. Mix the ham with the raw pork, beef or turkey, graham cracker crumbs, milk and ketchup. Roll into 1 1/4" balls. Place in a 9 x 13" pan.

4. Mix the 2nd group of ingredients together in a separate bowl or measuring cup to make the sauce. Pour over the top of the meatballs, making sure to cover each one.

5. Bake for 50 minutes or until the internal temperature reaches 160°.

Corn Dogs

Fried golden and crispy, kids love corn dogs!

1 c flour
1/2 c cornmeal
2 tbsp sugar
1/2 tsp baking soda (not powder)

3/4 c milk
2 tbsp oil

8 hot dogs
4 c oil for frying

1. Place the oil in a deep fryer, electric frying pan with high sides, or a small saucepan. Begin heating to 350°*.

2. Mix the flour, cornmeal, sugar, and baking soda together in a bowl. Add the milk and oil and stir well.

3. Dry hot dogs with a paper towel. Insert a popsicle stick in the end.

4. Dip the hot dogs in the cornmeal batter and roll to coat completely.

5. Once the oil has come up to temperature, drop the coated hot dogs into the oil 2 at a time. Turn a few times while cooking so they brown evenly. Fry until golden brown, approximately 5 minutes.

6. Remove with tongs. Place on a plate lined with paper towels to cool a little.

These can be microwaved, but they won't turn out perfectly round or crispy.

It is best to use an inexpensive candy thermometer or an electric deep fryer to make sure the temperature is right. If you don't have either, test the oil by putting a drop of batter in the oil. When it bubbles rapidly it is hot enough, but do not allow the oil to become so hot as to put off a strong oil smell into the air.

Fried Chicken

Some homemade fried chicken recipes do not include dipping the chicken in eggs first. But it is common when the recipe makes very crispy fried chicken. This recipe makes extra crispy chicken, especially when deep fried. Or, check the frozen food section of your grocery store. Most boxes of frozen fried chicken are egg-free.

3 lbs chicken legs, thighs, wings, or breasts cut into strips

1 c milk

1 c flour
1 c cornmeal
2 tsp salt
1 tsp onion powder
1 tsp baking soda
1/2 tsp black pepper

oil for frying

1. Pour at least 1" of oil into a large frying pan, or enough to cover the chicken if deep frying. Begin heating. For deep frying, heat the oil to 350°.

2. Pour the milk into a small flat bottomed pan.

3. Mix the second group of ingredients together in a flat bottomed pan.

4. Beginning with fairly dry pieces of chicken (dry with a paper towel if needed), dip the chicken in the milk, turning to coat both sides. Then place in the flour mixture and turn to coat.

5. Dip the piece back in the milk quickly, turning to wet both sides. Roll in the flour mixture a second time until completely coated.

6. Coat 1 piece of chicken at a time just before placing in the oil. Be careful not to overload the pan, which can make the temperature of the oil drop.

7. If pan frying, turn over when it becomes brown. Fry until a meat thermome-

ter should reads 185° at the bone. Drain on a plate lined with paper towels.

Try serving strips or wings with dipping sauce, such as Honey Mustard Dipping Sauce (page 82) or Ranch Dressing (page 72).

*Chicken tenderloins are the perfect size for chicken strips. Or, cut chicken breasts the long way to make 3 strips each.

This recipe is also makes wonderful fried fish. Thin fillets, such as whiting, can be breaded while still frozen and put into the fryer. They cook in less than 10 minutes. Break the fillets in half to fit them into a small deep fryer. Make sure they reach an internal temperature of 145° and flake easily with a fork.

Chicken Noodle Soup

Pasta makes a good alternative to egg noodles for soup. It does require some extended cooking time to make the noodles soft. A faster alternative is to make your chicken soup with instant rice or quick barley instead of noodles.

8 c water
4 oz fettuccini, linguini, or spaghetti*
2 tsp salt

48 oz chicken broth
2 carrots (optional)
2 stalks celery (optional)
1 onion (optional)
1 tbsp dried parsley (optional)

1. Bring the water to a boil. Pick up a few sticks of the pasta at a time. Start at one end and break off 1" pieces until all 4 oz have been broken. (Larger pieces will be to hard to keep a spoon.)

2. Add the salt and pasta to the boiling water. Stir well to make sure the pieces stay separated. Cover and cook on medium heat for 20 minutes. Drain.

3. Pour the broth into a large stock pot and bring to a boil. Add the pasta.

4. Chop or shred the carrots and celery, press or mince the garlic and add.

5. Cook for 10 minutes or until the vegetables are tender. Stir the parsley in just before serving.

The pasta can be cooked directly in the chicken broth. Because it absorbs a large quantity of liquid, it is less expensive and easier to control the balance of noodles to liquid by cooking the pasta first.

*The wide pastas look more like traditional egg noodles than spaghetti, but they must cook longer to become soft.

Dumplings for Soup

Light and fluffy, dumplings are another alternative to using egg noodles in soup. Recipes for dumplings sometimes call for an egg, and sometimes they do not. Here is an egg-free version if your cookbook at home includes an egg.

3/4 c flour
1/4 tsp baking soda (not powder)
1/8 tsp salt
1 tbsp dried parsley (optional)

1/4 c milk
2 tbsp oil

1. Bring the soup to boiling.

2. Mix the flour, baking soda, and salt together. Add the milk and oil all at once. Stir until just combined.

3. Drop rounded tablespoons of dough into the boiling soup (about 6 dumplings total).

4. Cover with a tight fitting lid. Lower the heat to medium or medium-low, enough to keep soup at a low boil.

5. Cook for 15 minutes. Do not lift the lid while cooking.

6. Serve immediately.

Lasagna

Frozen lasagnas usually come egg-free. But they often leave much to be desired in terms of taste and texture compared to homemade lasagna. Your favorite lasagna recipe will work perfectly if you use the following cheese mixture instead of mixing an egg with ricotta as is usual.

1 - 15 oz tub ricotta cheese
1 c mozzarella cheese
1/4 c grated parmesan

1. Mix the cheeses together.
2. Prepare lasagna according to the directions on the box of pasta. Add in the cheese mixture in the center layer of noodles instead of the cheese mixture with egg.
3. Bake according to directions on the box of lasagna.

Alternative: In place of ricotta and egg or the above mixture, spread each layer of lasagna noodles with cottage cheese, cover with mozzarella and sprinkle with parmesan.

White Pizza Sauce

Popular in some regions of the country, white sauce is used in place of tomato sauce on pizzas, especially for toppings that go well with the taste of Alfredo, like chicken or spinach. This recipe makes just the right amount of sauce for one large pizza.

2 tbsp oil
2 tbsp flour

1 c milk

1 tbsp parmesan
1/2 tsp garlic salt
1/4 tsp oregano
black pepper

1. In a small saucepan, heat the oil. Mix in the flour and stir until browned.

2. Add the milk slowly, whisking until it is incorporated with the oil and flour.

3. Add the seasonings and simmer until thick and bubbly.

Alfredo Sauce

A few bottled brands do not contain eggs, but most do so look carefully or create this easy sauce at home.

1/4 c butter
2 cloves garlic

2 c (1 pint) half & half or milk
2 tbsp cornstarch
1/4 tsp garlic salt

1/3 c parmesan cheese

2 tsp dried parsley (optional)

1. In a heavy saucepan, melt the butter over low heat. Press or crush and finely chop the garlic and sauté lightly without browning.

2. In a measuring cup, mix the half & half or milk with the cornstarch and garlic salt. Stirring until smooth, then add to the butter. Cook over medium-low heat, stirring until thick and bubbly.

3. Stir in the parmesan and parsley, if desired, and serve.

Provides enough sauce for 1 pound of pasta. Creamiest when made with half and half.

Side Dishes

&

Miscellaneous

Sweet Potato Casserole

Sweet potatoes can be baked without eggs, but they lack the custardy consistency of a casserole. This holiday favorite can be prepared in the oven, microwave, or even a crock pot if your oven is full during the holidays.

60 ounces canned sweet potatoes

1/4 c milk
1 tbsp cornstarch
1 tsp cinnamon
1/2 tsp salt
1/4 tsp nutmeg

2 tbsp orange juice concentrate
2 tbsp melted butter
mini marshmallows or pecan halves

1. Preheat the oven to 350° (unless preparing in a crockpot).

2. Drain the sweet potatoes. Beat with an electric mixer until smooth. Long fibers from the sweet potatoes will collect around the beaters. Discard them.

3. Combine in the 2nd group of ingredients together,. Add to the sweet potatoes and mix in. Add the butter and orange juice and mix in.

4. Grease a 2 quart casserole dish or medium sized crock pot. Add the sweet potato mixture. If baking in the oven, top with marshmallows or pecans.

5. Bake for 1 hour uncovered in a 325-350° oven, microwave for 10 minutes, or heat in the crockpot set on low for 4 or more hours. For the microwave or crockpot method, move to a serving dish after cooking and add the topping. Bake on the highest rack for 10 minutes or broil to toast the topping.

Pecan halves look nice placed tightly around the outside edges pointing in toward the center of the dish, or they can be chopped and sprinkled over the entire top. The recipe can be doubled and cooked in a large crock pot.

Scalloped Corn

The corn flavor really pops in this version of a creamy classic side dish.

2- 14.75 oz cans creamed corn
2 tbsp melted butter
1/4 c milk*

1/2 c cornmeal
1/4 tsp baking soda (not powder)

1. Preheat the oven to 350°.
2. Grease a 1 1/2 quart casserole dish.
3. Combine the corn, butter, and milk in the casserole dish.
4. In a separate bowl, mix the cornmeal and baking soda together. Add to the creamed corn and mix well.
5. Bake for 60 minutes or microwave for 10 minutes (baking gives the best result).

*To make an extra creamy version, add an extra 2 tablespoons of milk.

Variation: 1 lb of frozen broccoli can be use in place of 1 of the cans of creamed corn. Heath the broccoli in the microwave until hot (5 minutes) and salt well before adding to the corn.

Breading for Baking

This quick, healthy alternative to deep frying produces great crunch and flavor for a lot less work and calories. It works well on chicken and fish.

3 c corn flakes cereal
1 tsp garlic salt
1/2 tsp onion powder
1 tsp paprika
several shakes cayenne
several shakes black pepper
3 tbsp oil

1. Preheat the oven to 400°.
2. Crush the corn flakes by placing them in a large zip bag and rolling over them with a rolling pin or placing them in a food processor.
3. Mix the crumbs with the seasoning. Then drizzle the oil over the crumbs and stir well using your hands to distribute the oil evenly.
4. Roll any food that is slightly moist in the breading (dip in milk to moisten if needed) or lay the food items out on a cookie sheet and spoon the topping over it and pat it down slightly.
5. Bake as usually directed for the food selected. (Chicken breasts cut into strips 15-25 minutes at 350°, depending on the thickness, until they reach an internal temperature of 165°, etc)

This works especially well on any type of frozen white fish. Bake the filets for 10 minutes at 400°, drain the water that has been released into the pan, spoon the cornflake mixture over the top of each filet and bake another 10 minutes. From freezer to finished in 20 minutes! It's a healthy meal and the crunch is really satisfying.

Breading for Frying

Lots of yummy crunchy foods are breaded by dipping them in eggs, and then in some type of breadcrumb mixture. This makes most of the appetizer menu at restaurants off-limits to those who can't eat eggs. This versatile recipe will let you bread almost anything-from stuffed jalapenos to chicken strips, onion rings to mushrooms, string cheese to fried pickles.

1/2 c milk
1/2 c flour
1/4 tsp garlic salt
1/4 tsp onion powder
1/4 tsp baking powder
1/8 tsp black pepper
dash cayenne pepper

1 c Panko or regular breadcrumbs (Check the label-some contain eggs.)
1/2 tsp garlic salt
dash cayenne pepper

1. Mix together the first group of ingredients in a large flat-bottomed dish with sides, such as a pie plate.

2. In a separate dish, mix together the breadcrumbs and seasoning.

3. Dip the food you wish to fry in the milk mixture, then roll in the breadcrumbs.

4. Fry in 350° oil until the outside is brown and crisp and the inside registers the appropriate internal temperature (i.e. 170° for boneless chicken strips).

Fried Rice

This staple Chinese side dish makes a great main dish when diced cooked chicken is added.

6 c cooked rice

1 1/4 c frozen mixed veggies (small dice)

1 tbsp sesame oil
1 tbsp soy sauce
1 tsp onion powder
1/2 tsp garlic powder
1/4 tsp turmeric

1. Start with 6 cups of cooked white rice. (To make it, boil 3 1/2 c water, add 1 3/4 c long grain white rice and 1 tsp salt. Cover with a lid. Simmer on low for 20 minutes.)

2. In a small saucepan or the microwave, heat the veggies.

3. In a large fry pan, wok or small Dutch oven, heat the sesame oil on medium high. Add the other seasonings and stir to combine.

4. Add the rice and the veggies. Stir to coat and to keep from sticking.

5. Cook and stir until hot and slightly browned/crisp. This will only take about 2 minutes if you start with hot rice.

Eggnog

If you want a thick classic eggnog that will cling to your glass, give this egg-free version a try.

6 c milk (2% or whole)
1 - 3.4 oz package French vanilla instant pudding mix
1/2 tsp nutmeg
1/4 tsp salt

1. Whisk together or place in a container with a tightly fitting lid and shake to combine.

2. Refrigerate until chilled.

Milk Nog

The flavor of eggnog, but with less thickness, fat and calories. It's easy to mix a single glass for a refreshing pick-me-up or bedtime snack at any time of the year.

1 c milk or half and half
2 tsp honey
dash nutmeg
pinch salt
few drops vanilla extract (optional)
dash turmeric spice for color (optional)

1. Mix together in a serving glass and enjoy!

Desserts

Chocolate Chip Cookies

Classic chewy chocolate cookies with a touch of crispness around the edges. The pumpkin does not add any flavor to the cookie dough or baked cookies so no one will notice. And since there are no eggs, it its safe to lick the beaters!

1 c butter
1 c brown sugar
1/2 c canned pumpkin
1 tsp vanilla

2 c flour
1 tsp baking soda (not powder)
1 tsp salt

1/2 a package of chocolate chips

1. Preheat the oven to 350°.

2. Cream the butter and sugar together with an electric mixer. Add the pumpkin and vanilla and beat again until smooth.

3. In a separate bowl, stir the dry ingredients together. Add to the creamed butter and sugar and mix until well combined.

4. Stir in the chocolate chips with a large spoon until evenly mixed throughout the dough.

5. Drop by rounded teaspoonfuls on a cookie sheet. Bake for 20 minutes.

6. Place the cookie sheets on wire racks to cool. Once the cookies have cooled some, but are still slightly warm, remove them from the pan with a spatula and place them on a wire rack or plate.

Sugar Cookies

Break out the cookie cutters! These classic cookies can be cut into shapes and decorated for almost any occasion.

1 c butter
1 c sugar
2 tbsp milk
1 tsp vanilla

3 c flour
1/2 tsp baking powder
1/2 tsp baking soda
1/2 tsp salt

1. Cream the butter, sugar, milk, and vanilla.

2. Stir the dry ingredients together, and add to the bowl. Mix until combined and creamy.

3. Divide the dough into 2 balls. Place in plastic wrap and refrigerate for 30 minutes or more.

4. Preheat the oven to 375°.

5. On a floured surface, roll out one of the balls of dough to 1/4" thickness. Cut with cookie cutters.

6. Place on a greased cookie sheet. Bake for 10-12 minutes. Do not brown.

7. Cool the pan on a wire rack. Once the cookies have cooled enough that they hold together when being moved, use a spatula to move them to a wire rack or plate.

8. Decorate with icing if desired.

Peanut Butter Cookies

Try these plain or with a chocolate kiss added on top.

1 c brown sugar
1/2 c creamy peanut butter
1/2 c salted butter

1/4 c milk
1 tsp vanilla

1 1/2 c flour
1 tsp baking soda (not powder)
1/2 tsp salt

1. Preheat the oven to 375°.

2. Cream the brown sugar, peanut butter and butter together. Add the milk and vanilla and beat until fluffy.

3. Stir the dry ingredients together, and add to the bowl. Mix until combined.

4. Roll into 1" balls. Roll in sugar to create a crisp outer coating.

5. Place on an ungreased cookie sheet at least 2" apart. Flatten with a fork in 2 directions to make a crisscross pattern. Or, do not flatten and press a chocolate kiss into the top of each cookie.

6. Bake 8-10 minutes.

7. Cool the pan on a wire rack until the cookies are just warm. Then move the cookies to a wire rack or a plate.

Oatmeal Cookies

Chewy-crisp cookies with a little cinnamon flavor.

1/2 c salted butter
1/2 c sugar
1/2 c brown sugar
2 tbsp milk
1 tsp vanilla

3/4 c flour
1 tsp baking soda (not powder)
1/2 tsp cinnamon (optional)
1/4 tsp salt

1 1/2 c uncooked quick oats

1. Preheat the oven to 375°.

2. Cream the 1st group of ingredients.

3. Combine the 2nd group of ingredients, add them to the creamed ingredients and mix until creamy. Stir in the oats.

4. Drop rounded teaspoons of dough on greased cookie sheet 3" apart. Flatten a little with the back of the spoon or the bottom of a drinking glass or by pressing lightly with your fingers.

5. Bake for 10 minutes for a chewy center, or 12 minutes for a crisp cookie.

6. Remove the cookies from the oven and place the pan on a wire rack. Let the pan cool for a few minutes. Once the cookies have cooled enough so they hold together, use a spatula to move them to a wire rack to cool.

Add extra flavor and texture by adding 1/2 cup of: raisins, chopped walnuts or pecans, coconut flakes, or Grape-Nuts® cereal for super crisp cookies.

Makes 2 dozen cookies.

Snickerdoodles

These cinnamon sugar crackle top cookies are always a hit. And because this dough is slightly thicker than standard recipes with an egg, it isn't necessary to chill the dough before rolling and baking!

3/4 c sugar
1/2 c salted butter
1/4 c milk
1 tsp vanilla

1 1/2 c flour
2 tbsp cornstarch
1 tsp cream of tartar
3/4 tsp baking soda (not powder)
1/4 tsp salt

2 tbsp sugar
2 tsp cinnamon

1. Preheat the oven to 375°.

2. Cream the butter and sugar together. Add the milk and vanilla and beat until creamy.

3. In a separate bowl, stir the 2nd group of ingredients together. Then add to the creamed ingredients. Mix well until combined.

4. Mix the sugar and cinnamon together in a small bowl.

5. Scoop out level tablespoons of dough. Roll between the palms of your hands to make 1 inch balls. Roll in the cinnamon sugar.

6. Place on an ungreased cookie sheet 2" apart. Bake 10 minutes.

7. Cool the pan on a wire rack. Once the cookies have cooled enough that they hold together, use a spatula to move them to a wire rack or plate.

Chocolate Chocolate Chip Cookies

Double chocolate cookies that are fabulously melty inside. If you like chocolate mint, you have to try making these with Crème de menthe chips.

1 c brown sugar
1/2 c butter
1/2 c pumpkin
1 tsp vanilla

1 3/4 c flour
1/4 c cocoa powder
1/2 tsp baking soda (not powder)
1/2 tsp salt

2 tbsp milk

1/2 c Chocolate Chips or Andes® Crème de Menthe baking chips
(or finely chopped Andes® mints)

1. Preheat the oven to 350°.
2. Cream the 1st group of ingredients with an electric mixer.
3. In a separate bowl, mix the 2nd group of ingredients together, then add to the creamed sugar and butter. Mix until combined.
4. Add the milk and beat until creamy.
5. Stir in the chocolate chips, crème de menthe chips or chopped mints.
6. Drop by rounded teaspoonful on a greased cookie sheet. Bake 20 minutes.

Allow the pan to cool for several minutes on a wire rack. Once the cookies have cooled enough that they don't fall apart, move them with a spatula to a wire rack. Once cool, store them in a container that is not airtight (or place the lid on top but do not seal it) to help retain the appropriate level of moisture.

Spritz Cookies

These detailed shaped cookies made with a cookie press are common around Christmas and the holidays.

3/4 c salted butter
1/2 c sugar
2 tbsp milk
1/2 tsp almond or vanilla extract

1 3/4 c flour
2 tbsp cornstarch
1/2 tsp baking soda (not powder)
1/4 tsp salt

1. Preheat the oven to 375°.
2. Cream the 1st group of ingredients together in a bowl using an electric mixer.
3. In a separate bowl, mix together the 2nd group of ingredients. Add to the creamed ingredients and mix until well combined.
4. Put the dough into a cookie press. Press onto an ungreased cookie sheet. Apply just enough dough to form the shape of the cookie. Space the cookies at least 1" between they will spread a little.
5. Bake for 8 minutes. Cool the pan on a wire rack until the cookies are cool.

Sprinkles can be added before baking.

Mexican Wedding Cakes

Mexican wedding cakes, also known as Russian tea cakes, are a powdery white cookie that melts in your mouth. They are one of the few cookie recipes that are usually made without eggs. This version is included to make you aware of these egg-free cookies and to offer a cookie with a different texture.

1 c flour
1/2 c powdered sugar
1/2 c cornstarch

3/4 c butter
1 tsp vanilla

1/2 c finely chopped walnuts or pecans

powdered sugar

1. Preheat the oven to 350°

2. Combine the 1st three ingredients.

3. Mix in the butter using an electric mixer. Add the vanilla and mix in.

4. Roll into 1" balls. Roll in powdered sugar and place on a ungreased cookie sheet. Refrigerate if needed to make the dough easy to handle. (Placing half of the dough in the fridge while working the 1st half works well.)

5. Bake 10-12 minutes.

6. Cool before serving.

Fudge Brownies

These brownies are a thrill for people who have been missing out the gooey texture and full fudge flavor of classic brownies. If you have tried vegan brownie recipes or attempted to substitute out eggs in the past with less than satisfying results, rest assured that this recipe will not disappoint.

1 c (6 ounces) semi-sweet chocolate chips

3 tbsp oil

1/2 c water
1 c brown sugar
1 tsp vanilla

1 1/2 c flour
2 tsp cornstarch
1 tsp baking powder
1/2 tsp salt

1. Grease an 8x8 glass pan or a 9x9 metal pan(glass produces the best result). Preheat the oven to **325° for glass or 350° for metal.**

2. Measure the chocolate chips (pat down in the cup). Place in a large microwave safe bowl. Microwave 1 minute. Stir. Microwave an additional 15 seconds and stir, repeating until melted. Add the oil and stir until smooth.

3. In a separate bowl, mix together the water, brown sugar and vanilla and stir until all lumps are gone. Add to the chocolate and mix in. The mixture will be a very runny liquid at this point.

4. In a separate bowl, mix together the dry ingredients in the last group. Add to the chocolate mixture and stir until combined. Pour into the pan.

5. Run the spatula or spoon from side to side across the top of the batter to make swirls. Bake 40 minutes for glass pans or 30 minutes for metal. (A toothpick inserted in the center will still show a little batter on the tip.)

6. Allow to cool before cutting. Cover as soon as they have cooled.

Cake Style Brownies

Brownies are so popular that several varieties exist. These are softer and lighter version than fudge brownies in terms of both texture and calories.

1 1/2 c flour
1 1/2 c brown sugar
1/2 c cocoa powder
1 tbsp cornstarch
1 tsp baking powder
1 tsp salt

1 c water
1/4 c oil
1 tsp vanilla

1. Preheat the oven to 350°. Grease the bottom and corners of a 9 x 13 pan.

2. Combine the 1st group of ingredients in a large bowl.

3. Measure the 2nd group of ingredients in a liquid measuring cup. Add to the dry ingredients all at once.

4. Stir well until most of the sugar lumps are gone. (Brown sugar has a tendency to clump, but it also adds more moisture to the recipe.)

5. Pour into the 9 x 13 pan. Bake 30 minutes, or until a toothpick inserted in the center comes out clean.

6. Allow to cool for a few minutes before cutting. Cover as soon as they have cooled.

These are great served slightly warm-especially with ice cream!

Blondies

Blondies are similar to brownies but taste a little like caramel instead of chocolate.

1 c brown sugar
1/2 c butter
1/4 c milk
1 tsp vanilla

2 c flour
1/4 tsp baking soda (not powder)
1/4 tsp salt

1. Preheat the oven to 350°. Grease an 8 x 8 pan.

2. Melt the butter in a large saucepan on the stove. Remove from heat.

3. Stir in the sugar, milk, and vanilla.

4. In a separate bowl, mix together the flour, salt, and baking soda. Add the melted butter and sugar mixture. Stir to combine.

5. Pour into the pan and spread out. Bake for 30 minutes.

Variations: Stir in 1 c of chocolate chips and/or 1/2 c of chopped walnuts or pecans before baking.

Any Cake Mix

A boxed cake mix can be modified using the following steps. The cake recipes in this cookbook are as easy to make as this recipe that uses a box of cake mix. So you might give one of them a try, even if you haven't had much experience or luck baking a cake from scratch in the past.

1 boxed cake mix (make sure it does not contain eggs)
6 tbsp cornstarch
1 tsp baking soda (not powder)

oil and water as directed on the box

If the box calls for 3 eggs:	**If the box calls for 3 egg whites:**
1/2 c milk	1/3 c milk
2 tbsp oil	

1. Preheat the oven and grease and flour the pans as directed on the box.

2. Pour the cake mix into a large bowl. Add the cornstarch and baking soda and mix well.

3. Measure the milk, and oil if needed. Add along with the oil and water as directed on the box. Beat according to the directions on the box.

4. Bake as directed on the box.

An alternative is to add 1 can of soda pop to a box mix and nothing else (none of the water or oil called for on the package) and bake according to the instructions on the box. Lemon-lime flavors work well for white and fruit-flavored cakes, and cola works well for chocolate cakes.

Altitude adjustments have not been tested. If you can provide input on how these recipes work at high-altitude, please email littlethingsbooks@gmail.com.

White Cake

It took lots of testing to create this recipe, but it is so easy to make.

1 1/2 c flour
1 c sugar
2 tsp cornstarch
1 tsp baking powder
1/2 tsp baking soda
1/2 tsp salt

3/4 c water
1/4 c oil
1 tbsp lemon juice
1 tsp vanilla

1. Preheat the oven to 350°. Generously grease a 9" round cake pan and dust with flour, or fill 12 cupcake tins with liners.

2. Mix the dry ingredients in a bowl. Stir with a whisk until very well mixed.

3. Measure the liquid ingredients, placing them all in the same measuring cup.

4. Pour the liquid ingredients into the dry ingredients. Mix with the whisk just until combined. (It is not better to use a mixer as it is for cakes with eggs.)

5. Pour into the pan and spread out. Bake for 25 minutes until a toothpick inserted in the center comes out clean. (8" pans may take 27-30 minutes).

6. Place on a wire rack. Cool completely. Loosen the edges with a knife before removing from the pan. Frost as desired.

Cupcakes: Fill 12 cupcake tins, bake 20 min.

9 x 13 Sheet Cake: Double the recipe. Grease the bottom of the pan only and do not flour. Bake 30 minutes.

Note: If baking several pans in the oven at once, or using 8" round pans the baking time may need to be increased by up to 5 minutes.

Chocolate Cake

Birthday cake can be a major challenge for families dealing with an egg allergy. But no one will feel like they are missing out when this moist chocolate cake is served! The secret ingredient works better than anything else tested and no one can ever seem to guess what it is.

1 1/2 c flour
1 1/4 c sugar
1/2 c cocoa powder
2 tsp cornstarch
2 tsp baking powder
1/2 tsp baking soda
3/4 tsp salt

1 c minus 1 tbsp canned pumpkin*
3/4 c water
1/2 c oil
1 tsp vanilla

1. Preheat the oven to 350°. Prepare the pans. Either grease and flour 2 - 9" round cake pans, or grease the bottom of a 9 x 13 glass pan and do not flour, or place paper liners in 18 cupcake spaces.

2. Combine the 1st group of ingredients in a large bowl. In a separate bowl, mix the 2nd group of ingredients together. Add to the dry ingredients and stir well with a spoon until the lumps are gone.

3. Pour into the pan(s) or cupcake liners. Spread flat with a spatula. Bake 25 minutes for cakes, or 20 minutes for cupcakes or until a toothpick inserted in the center comes out clean.

4. Allow to cool completely on wire racks. Frost as desired.

A great alternative to heavy sugary frosting? Cool whip®!

*Removing 1 tbsp makes the recipe use one half of a 15 oz can. This makes it easy to make a double batch, or to save just the right amount for a another cake later. To store, put in a plastic sandwich baggie, spread flat and freeze.

Yellow Cake

A very easy and quick cake.

1 1/2 c flour
3/4 c sugar
2 tsp cornstarch
1 tsp baking powder
1/2 tsp salt

1/2 c water
1/2 c oil
1/4 c orange juice
1 tsp vanilla

1. Preheat the oven to 350°. Generously grease a 9" round cake pan and dust with flour, or fill 12 cupcake tins with liners.

2. Mix the dry ingredients in a bowl. Stir with a whisk until very well mixed.

3. Measure the liquid ingredients, placing them all in the same measuring cup.

4. Pour the liquid ingredients into the dry ingredients. Mix with the whisk just until combined. (Do not use a mixer and beat for a long time like cakes with eggs.)

5. Pour into the pan and spread out. Bake for 25 minutes until a toothpick inserted in the center comes out clean.

6. Place on a wire rack. Cool completely. Loosen the edges with a knife before removing from the pan. Frost as desired.

Cupcakes: Fill 12 cupcake tins, bake 20 min.

9 x 13 Sheet Cake: Double the recipe. Grease the bottom of the pan only and do not flour. Bake 30 minutes.

Note: If baking several pans in the oven at once, or using 8" round pans the baking time may need to be increased by up to 5 minutes.

Pineapple Upside-Down Cake

Beautiful and extra moist with a gooey caramel-like topping.

1/3 c brown sugar
2 tbsp melted butter
1 tbsp water

1 15 oz can sliced pineapple
maraschino cherry halves

1 c flour
2 tbsp cornstarch
2 tsp baking powder
1/2 tsp baking soda
1/4 tsp salt

3/4 c brown sugar
2/3 c applesauce
1/3 c oil

1. Preheat the oven to 350°.
2. Mix the first group of ingredients together in an ungreased 9" round cake pan.
3. Line the bottom of the pan with 7 pineapple slices until the bottom of the pan is full. Place a cherry in the center of each pineapple ring.
4. In a bowl, mix the third group of ingredients together. Mix the fourth group of ingredients together in a liquid measuring cup. Pour over the flour mixture and mix just until the lumps are gone. Gently pour and spoon over the pineapple rings.
5. Bake 35 minutes or until a toothpick inserted in the center comes out clean.
6. Cool for 10 minutes. Run a knife around the outside edge of the cake. Invert onto a cake plate.

Carrot Cake

Classic in every way-except no eggs!

2 1/2 c flour
2 tsp baking soda (not powder)
1 tsp cinnamon
1/2 tsp salt

2 c applesauce
2 c brown sugar
1/2 c oil

2 c shredded carrots (3-5 carrots)
1 c raisins (optional)
1 c chopped nuts (optional)

1. Preheat the oven to 350°. Grease and flour 2 - 9" round pans, or grease the bottom only of a 9x13 pan and do not flour.

2. Shred the carrots using the large hole on a shredder.

3. Combine the 1st group of ingredients in a large bowl. Mix the 2nd group of ingredients together, then add to the bowl. Stir with a spoon just until combined. Do not mix a long time like traditional cake recipes.

4. Add the carrots to the batter and fold in, along with the raisins and nuts if desired.

5. Pour into the prepared pans. Bake 30-35 minutes for round pans, and 40-45 minutes for a 9x13, or until a toothpick inserted in the center comes out clean.

6. Allow to cool completely on wire racks. Cut around the edges with a knife and invert onto a cake plate. Frost as desired.

Pumpkin Spice Cake

This cake can be served with a sugary crumb topping, cream cheese frosting or just a dusting of powdered sugar.

2 c flour
2 1/2 tsp pumpkin pie spice
2 tsp baking powder
1/2 tsp baking soda
3/4 tsp salt

1 c canned pumpkin
1 c brown sugar
3/4 c water
1/2 c oil

Crumb Topping:
1/2 c brown sugar
1/2 c flour
1/4 c butter
1/2 tsp pumpkin pie spice
1/4 tsp salt
1/2 c chopped walnuts or pecans (optional)

1. Preheat the oven to 350°. Grease the bottom of a 9 x 13 pan.

2. Combine the 1st group of ingredients in a large bowl. In a separate bowl, mix the 2nd group of ingredients together, then add to the flour mixture. Stir well with a spoon just until the lumps are removed. Pour into the pan.

3. Put in the oven. Set a timer for 25 minutes if baking without the topping, 30 minutes if adding the crumb topping. If adding the crumb topping, mix the ingredients together and cut in the butter with a fork until it resembles sand. As soon as it is mixed, gently remove the cake from the oven and sprinkle the topping over it evenly. Do not pat it down. Put the cake back in the oven and let it finish baking. (Bake 30-35 minutes total for cake with crumb topping or until a toothpick inserted in the center comes out clean).

Angel Food Cake

My grandmother often served this light and spongy cake, made almost entirely from egg whites, with strawberries and whipped cream covering the top. A surprisingly good substitute is found ready-made in the bakery isle. It makes it easy to create 1 serving of dessert for the person with an egg allergy.

1 loaf fresh French or Italian bread

frozen sliced strawberries in sugar

whipped cream (page 151) or Cool Whip®

1. Thaw the strawberries and the Cool Whip®.

2. Slice a 2-4" thick piece of bread for each serving needed. A wedge shape can be cut to mimic the shape of angel food cake baked in a round pan if desired by alternating cutting the bread at an angle and cutting it straight.

3. Cut off the crust on all sides, sawing gently with a serrated knife to keep from smashing the edges of the bread.

4. Lay the slice down flat on a serving plate (instead of having it stand up) and cover most of the top with strawberries, including lots of juice to soak into the bread. Leave the corners white to show the "cake".

5. Add a generous dollop of Cool Whip® or whipped cream (page 151).

6. Serve, and see if they can figure out your secret!

Peach Cobbler

Many people enjoy warm fruit cobbler served with ice cream. Another amazing way to serve cobbler is to drizzle cream over the top. Once you try it, you will insist everyone you serve it to try it as well!

2 - 29 oz cans peaches in light syrup

1/4 c sugar
2 tbsp cornstarch
1 tsp cinnamon
1/4 tsp salt

2 1/2 c flour
1/2 c sugar
1 tsp baking soda (not powder)
1/2 tsp cinnamon
1/4 tsp salt

1 c milk
2 tbsp oil

1. Preheat the oven to 400°

2. Drain the peaches, reserving 1/2 cup of the juice. Mix the 2nd group of ingredients into the 1/2 cup of juice.

3. Spread the peaches out in a 9" x 13" glass pan. Pour the juice mixture over the top of the peaches.

4. Combine the 3rd group of ingredients. Mix the milk and oil together. Pour over the dry ingredients. Mix just until combined.

5. Drop large spoonfuls of the batter (about 9) over the top of the peaches.

6. Bake for 35 minutes.

Strawberry Shortcake

Forming individual shortcakes allows for quicker cooking time and a better crust on each serving. They look beautiful when sliced and layered with strawberries inside and on top. The batter goes together incredibly fast and can be baked ahead of time, so it's perfect for company either way.

**1 - 16 oz container frozen sweetened strawberries
   (or 2 cups sliced fresh strawberries + 1/4 c sugar)**

**2 1/2 c flour
1/4 c sugar
1/2 tsp salt
1 tsp baking soda (not powder)**

**2/3 c milk
1/3 c oil***

1. Thaw the frozen strawberries or slice the fresh strawberries and sprinkle with 1/4 c sugar.

2. Preheat oven to 350°.

3. Combine the 1st group of ingredients in a large bowl.

4. Pour the milk into a liquid measuring cup. Measure the oil by adding it on top of the milk (measures to the 1 cup mark when placed together).

5. Pour the milk and oil over the dry ingredients all at once. Gently stir by making small circles with a fork and then folding with a spatula until just barely combined. A little dry flour can remain.

6. Using a soup spoon (the larger sized spoon in a silverware set), drop heaping spoonfuls of batter on an ungreased cookie sheet. Gently round the sides with fingers if desired.

7. Bake for 15 minutes for soft shortcakes, 20 minutes for a little crunch on the outer texture that provides a nice compliment to the soft strawberries.

Allow to cool for a few minutes before serving. Split the shortcakes in half lengthwise, fill the center with strawberries and spoon strawberries over the top to create a layered dessert. Add whipped cream if desired (page 151).

If baking ahead of time, do not store an airtight container. Cool completely and cover with a clean towel, or place in a gallon size food storage bag left unsealed with the top folded over. Wait to fill with strawberries until just before serving.

*Believe it or not, extra virgin olive oil tastes bests in this recipe. It adds a delightful, complex flavor to the dessert, as well as a little color that makes it look as if eggs were added.

Lemon Bars

Sweet, tart and colorful. Who can resist this popular treat? Usually, only people who can't eat eggs. But not with this recipe!

1/3 c butter
1/4 c sugar
1 c flour

1/4 c butter

1 1/2 c water
1 1/2 c sugar
3/4 c cornstarch
1/2 c lemon juice
1 tbsp lemon zest (optional)

1. Preheat oven to 350°.

2. Combine the 1st group of ingredients using an electric mixer, pastry cutter or fork.

3. Press into the bottom of a 8 x 8 glass pan.

4. Bake for 20 minutes.

5. Meanwhile, place the 1/4 cup butter in a small saucepan. Melt over medium heat.

6. Mix the remaining ingredients together in a separate bowl, then add to the melted butter in the pan. Whisk continually over medium heat until thick and bubbly.

7. Pour over the hot crust. Allow to cool thoroughly.

8. Dust with powdered sugar if desired. Cut into squares using a sharp knife.

Key Lime Pie

This is as quick and easy as baking a pie from scratch can get.

2 - 14 oz cans sweetened condensed milk
1/2 c sour cream
1/2 c key lime juice

1 - 9" graham cracker crust*

1. Preheat oven to 350°.

2. Stir together the 1st group of ingredients using a whisk.

3. Pour into a prepared graham cracker crust. Do not over fill. Depending on the brand of crust used, a small amount of filling may be left over.

4. Bake for 8 minutes on a cookie sheet. The pie will not look much different. Remove and allow to cool to room temperature.

Add whipped cream if desired (page 151).

***Graham Cracker Crust:** Purchase a large ready-made graham cracker crust or make one by doing the following: Grind 18 graham crackers in a food processor, add 1/4 c sugar and 1/3 c melted butter. Combine well, press into a pie plate and chill in the refrigerator, covered, for at least 1 hour.

Lemon Meringue Pie

This no-bake pie is easy to whip up. A great summertime treat!

1 - 9" baked pie crust

1 c sugar
3/4 c lemon juice
3/4 c water
1/4 c cornstarch
1/4 salt
1 drop yellow food coloring* (optional)

2 tbsp salted butter

Meringue for Pie (page 139)

1. Bake a pie crust, or use a graham cracker crust, or make this a crustless pie by pouring the lemon filling directly into an ungreased pie plate.

2. Combine the 2nd group of ingredients in a small saucepan. Stir thoroughly to mix in the cornstarch using a whisk. Place over medium heat. Stir occasionally until it begins to steam. Then reduce to medium-low and stir constantly until thick and bubbly-about 10-12 minutes total. Remove from heat.

3. Stir in the butter. Pour into the pie crust or plate. Refrigerate (cover with a bowl turned upside down to protect it from odors) for 45 minutes–1 hour.

4. If moisture beads have formed on the pie in the refrigerator, remove them by gently dabbing a flat paper towel on the top.

5. Follow the directions for making the meringue (page 139).

* The lemon filling will be light yellow without coloring. If your food coloring bottle does not have a dropper top, add the coloring to the water before mixing it with anything else. If it looks orange, add more water until it turns yellow. Then dump out all but 3/4 cup and use that in the recipe.

Meringue for Pie

This pie topping can be made far faster than the classic version made almost entirely from egg whites. It also does not require any baking time!

2 envelopes unflavored gelatin
1 c water
1/2 c sugar

1 tsp vanilla extract
1/8 tsp salt
vanilla extract for color

1. Prepare the pie and bake if required. Cool completely.

2. Pour the water into a small saucepan. Sprinkle the gelatin over the top. Allow to set for 1 minute until moistened.

3. Add the sugar to the center of the saucepan and stir lightly until the sugar is under the water. Place the pan over medium heat.

4. As soon as the mixture begins to simmer, remove it from the heat. Pour into a mixing bowl and stir in the vanilla and salt. Allow to cool until the bowl is only slightly warm to the touch-about 15 minutes. (Do not refrigerate).

5. With an electric mixer, beat on high speed about 7 minutes until the mixer leaves swirled tracks in the meringue that do not fall flat.

6. Pour 1/2 of the mixture over the pie and spread out to edges of the crust. Then drop large dollops on top of the pie with a large spoon. Pull the spoon up out of the mixture to make peaks. Once the mix begins to set, continuing to try and lift peaks out of the top will make the top lumpy. Timing is key.

7. Allow to rest for 30 minutes to set. To make the edges of the meringue look browned, color them with vanilla extract. Dip your finger or the back of a metal spoon into the vanilla. Lightly stroke the top of the ridges and peaks, re-dipping it in the vanilla frequently until the top of the pie has the color variations of a lightly toasted marshmallow.

Banana Cream Pie

This stove top method goes together quickly. Rather skip the pie crust? Simply pour into individual serving dishes for a simple pudding snack.

**1 1/2 c milk
3 tbsp cornstarch
2 tbsp sugar
1/4 tsp salt**

**2 tbsp butter
1/2 tsp vanilla
2 medium bananas**

1 - 9" baked pie crust or graham cracker crust*

Meringue for Pie (page 139) or whipped cream (page 151)

1. Combine the 1st group of ingredients in a saucepan before placing over heat.

2. Cook on medium heat, stirring constantly. Once thick and bubbly, turn off heat and stir in butter and vanilla.

3. Slice the bananas 1/4" thick. Fold into the cream mixture.

4. Pour into the baked pie crust or graham cracker crust. Make sure each sliced banana on the top is covered with the cream mixture.

5. Cover and chill at least 30 minutes.

6. Top with meringue (page 139) or whipped cream (page 151).

*Purchase a large ready-made graham cracker crust or see recipe on page 137.

Coconut Cream Pie

This stove top method goes together quickly. Rather skip the pie crust? Simply pour into individual serving dishes for a simple pudding snack.

1 - 9" baked pie crust or graham cracker crust*

1 1/2 c coconut milk or milk
3 tbsp cornstarch
2 tbsp sugar
1/4 tsp salt

2 tbsp butter or coconut oil
1 c flaked sweetened coconut

Meringue for pie (page 139) or whipped cream (page 151)
2 tbsp toasted coconut (optional)**

1. Prepare a graham cracker crust or bake a pie crust according to package or recipe directions. Toast 2 tbsp of coconut by baking on a cookie sheet at 350° for 5-10 minutes, or by placing in a dry skillet over medium heat and stirring until it just begins to brown.

2. Stir the 2nd group of ingredients together in a saucepan. Place over medium heat. Stir constantly. Once thick and bubbly, remove from heat. Stir in the butter or coconut oil and the 1 c flaked sweetened coconut.

3. Pour into the pie crust. Cover and chill at least 30 minutes.

4. Top with egg-free meringue (recipe page 139) or whipped cream (page 151).

5. Sprinkle toasted coconut on top if desired.

*Purchase a ready-made graham cracker crust or see recipe on page 137.

Raisin Cream Pie

This is easy to make and looks impressive on a plate.

1 1/2 c raisins
1 - 14 oz can sweetened condensed milk
1/2 c sour cream
1 tsp vanilla extract
pinch of salt

1 - 9" unbaked pie crust

Meringue for pie (page 139)

1. Preheat oven to 350°.

2. Mix the 1st group of ingredients together in a large bowl. Pour into the pie crust.

3. Bake uncovered for 30 minutes. Allow the pie to cool.

4. Prepare the meringue (page 139). Drop big spoonfuls on top of the pie, creating large swirls and peaks. Let set for 30 minutes or until the meringue is firm.

5. To make the top of the meringue look toasted, lightly brush the ridges and peaks with the back of a spoon dipped in vanilla extract.

Chocolate Pudding

Commercially packaged pudding and pudding mixes do not typically contain eggs. But made from scratch pudding does. This recipe is nice to have in a pinch. It is also useful if you want, or need, to avoid artificial ingredients or make a dairy-free pudding using almond or soy milk.

3 c milk
3/4 c sugar
1/4 c cocoa powder
1/4 tsp salt

1/4 c cornstarch

1 tbsp salted butter
1 tsp vanilla extract

1. Pour 2 cups of the milk into a large saucepan. Begin heating on the stovetop on medium. Add the sugar and cocoa powder and mix in with a wire whisk.

2. Mix the cornstarch into the remaining 1 cup of milk. Once the milk on the stovetop begins to steam, add the milk with the cornstarch.

3. Stir constantly until thick and bubbly, about 2 more minutes.

4. Remove from heat.

5. Stir in the butter. Pour into 4 individual serving dishes or 1 large dish. Cover with plastic wrap to keep a skin from forming.

6. Refrigerate until cold, 45-60 minutes.

For extra rich dark chocolate pudding, melt 1 oz unsweetened bakers chocolate into the pudding along with the butter.

For pie filling, reduce the milk to 2 1/2 c. Fills 1 deep dish pie.

Tapioca Pudding

Cook n' serve boxes of tapioca pudding and premade pudding cups usually do not contain eggs. But if you only have good old fashioned tapioca on hand, or simply want to avoid artificial ingredients, use this recipe instead of the one on the box that requires eggs.

2 c milk
1/3 c sugar
4 tbsp minute tapioca
pinch salt

1. Mix the ingredients together in a small saucepan and let sit for 5 minutes.

2. Heat on medium, stirring frequently until bubbly.

3. Remove from the heat. (It will not thicken fully until it cools.)

4. Pour into serving dishes and allow to cool at least 20 minutes.

Bread Pudding

Don't have stale bread? Simply place fresh bread slices in the oven for 5 minutes while preheating, or run them through the toaster set on low to barely toast them.

4 slices stale bread

1 3/4 c milk
1/3 c sugar
3 tbsp cornstarch
2 tbsp melted butter
1/2 tsp cinnamon
1 tsp vanilla

1/3 c raisins

1. Preheat the oven to 350°.

2. Butter a 2 qt. casserole dish or a pie plate.

3. Mix the 2nd group of ingredients and stir well until the cornstarch is completely mixed in.

4. Stir in the raisins.

5. Dice the bread and spread it out in the pan. Pour the milk mixture over the top and fold gently.

6. Bake for 35 minutes.

Crème Brulee

This elegant custard is perfect for entertaining. Traditionally, the sugar topping is melted and browned with a torch. But this recipe eliminates the need for special equipment as well as a half a dozen egg yolks.

2 c half and half (approximately 1 pint)
1 - 2.9 oz box cook n' serve custard pudding mix*

2 tbsp white sugar
2 tbsp brown sugar

1. Mix the cream and custard mix in a heavy saucepan. Place over medium heat. Stir constantly until the sugar dissolves and the mixture is thick and bubbly.

2. Pour into a 1 quart oven proof dish or 4 small ramekins. Cover and refrigerate until chilled and set, at least 2 hours.

3. Combine the white and brown sugar. Sprinkle the sugar mix over the top of the chilled crème brulee. Allow it to sit a few minutes until the sugar becomes moist.

4. Position the top rack in the oven so the top of the custard will be 6" below the broiler. Turn the oven broiler on low. Place the crème brulee on the top oven rack and broil for 2-3 minutes. Watch carefully to prevent burning and remove as soon as the tops turn brown.

5. Immediately return the crème brulee to the refrigerator, uncovered, for at least 15 minutes to re-set.

Crème brulee is usually served chilled.

*Name brand boxed mixes are usually egg free, but check the label to be certain.

Cheesecake

Cheesecake is one treat that is tough to give up! Don't miss out. Anyone can make this easy egg-free version. It is as thick and rich as any cheesecake.

2 - 8 oz packages cream cheese

1/4 c water
1 envelope unflavored gelatin

1 c un-sifted powdered sugar
1 tsp vanilla extract or 1 tbsp lemon juice

1 - 9" graham cracker crust*

1. Remove cream cheese from refrigerator and allow to warm to room temperature.

2. Add the water to a microwave safe measuring cup or coffee mug. Sprinkle the gelatin over the water and let sit for 1 minute. Microwave for 30 seconds to dissolve. Allow to cool for 3-5 minutes until only slightly warm to the touch. Do not let it to begin to set before mixing with the cream cheese.

3. In a large bowl, beat the cream cheese with an electric mixer until smooth. Add the powdered sugar (measure like flour by sprinkling in the cup then leveling off), and vanilla or lemon juice. Beat on low until smooth. Pour in the gelatin mixture (do not scrape the sides of the container it was heated in as it may add clumps) and mix on low until combined.

4. Pour into the graham cracker crust. Cover and refrigerate until set (1-2 hours). For the best consistency, let the cheesecake sit out at room temperature for about 15 minutes before serving.

Pick your topping! A tablespoon of raspberry preserves or canned cherry pie filling or a drizzle of caramel or chocolate sauce make a perfect topping.
*Purchase a ready-made graham cracker crust see recipe page 137.

Chocolate Cheesecake

Rich and velvety. This easy dessert is a winner.

2 - 8 oz packages of cream cheese

1/2 c water
1 packet unflavored gelatin

1 1/4 c un-sifted powdered sugar
1/2 c cocoa powder
1/8 tsp salt

1 - 9" graham cracker crust*

1. Remove cream cheese from refrigerator and allow to warm to room temperature.

2. Add the water to a microwave safe measuring cup or coffee mug. Sprinkle the gelatin over the water and let sit for 1 minute. Microwave for 30 seconds to dissolve. Allow to cool for 3-5 minutes until only slightly warm to the touch. Do not let it to begin to set before mixing with the cream cheese.

3. In a large bowl, beat the cream cheese with an electric mixer until smooth. Add the powdered sugar (measure like flour by sprinkling in cup and leveling off) cocoa powder, and salt. Beat on low until smooth. Pour in the gelatin mixture (do not scrape the sides of the mug the gelatin was heated in as it may add clumps) and mix on low until combined.

4. Pour into graham cracker crust. Cover and refrigerate until set. (1-2 hours)

*Purchase a ready-made graham cracker crust or follow recipe on page 137.

Peanut Butter Pie

This pie is as rich and luscious as French silk pie, but it's peanut butter!

1/2 pint heavy whipping cream
2 tbsp un-sifted powdered sugar

1/2 c water
1 envelope unflavored gelatin

1 1/2 c creamy peanut butter
1 c powered sugar
1/2 c brown sugar
1/4 c salted butter
1 tsp vanilla

1 - 9" chocolate graham cracker pie crust

1. Whip the heavy whipping cream and powdered sugar in a small mixing bowl for 1-2 minutes until stiff peak stage is reached. Cover and refrigerate.

2. Add the water to a microwave safe measuring cup or coffee mug. Sprinkle the gelatin over the water and let sit for 1 minute. Microwave for 30 seconds to dissolve. Allow to cool for 3-5 minutes until only slightly warm to the touch.

3. In a large mixing bowl, add the 3rd group of ingredients and mix together with an electric mixer on low. Pour in the gelatin mixture (do not scrape the sides as it may add clumps) and beat on low until combined.

4. Reserve 1/2 cup of the whipped cream by placing it in a small plastic baggie. Add the remaining whipped cream. Mix in on low. Pour into the crust.

5. Cut a small tip off the corner of the plastic baggie and use it as a pastry bag to swirl 12 small rosettes around the outside edge of the pie. Refrigerate under a large bowl or in a cake carrier to protect the flavor from refrigerator odors for 2 hours or until firm.

6. Cut into 12 slices. Allow each slice to sit out a few minutes before serving.

French Silk Pie

Too perfect for words. It is just as velvety and rich as the famous pie served at restaurant chains known for their pie. It also goes together fast if you have a stand mixer and a prepared crust. No one should have to miss out on nothing-quite-as-good-as French silk pie due to a food allergy!

1 - 9" pie crust

1 - 4.4 oz bar of milk chocolate

1 - half pint heavy whipping cream*
2 tbsp powdered sugar

1/4 c water
1 packet unflavored gelatin

1/2 c salted butter
1 1/2 c powdered sugar
1/2 c cocoa powder

1. Bake a pie crust or prepare a graham cracker crust. Refrigerate.

2. Break the milk chocolate into pieces and place in a microwave safe bowl. Microwave on high 30 seconds, then stir. Repeat two more times or until melted. Set on the counter to cool.

3. Pour the heavy whipping cream into a small mixing bowl and add 2 tbsp powdered sugar (un-sifted-measure like flour). Whip on medium with an electric mixer for 2-3 minutes until stiff peaks form. Reserve 1/2 cup of the whipped cream for decorating the pie by placing it in a small plastic baggie or pastry bag and placing in the refrigerator.

4. Add the water to a microwave safe measuring cup or coffee mug. Sprinkle the gelatin over the water and let sit for 1 minute. Microwave for 30 seconds to dissolve. Allow to cool for 3-5 minutes until only slightly warm to the touch.

5. In a large mixing bowl, cream the softened butter. Add the powdered sugar (measure like flour by sprinkling in a measuring cup and leveling off) and cocoa powder and mix in on low. Add 2 tablespoons of the gelatin mixture (should be lukewarm) and mix in on low. Then mix in the melted chocolate, again on low.

6. Add the whipped cream from the bowl and mix it in on low. Pour into the prepared pie crust. Spread out evenly with a spatula.

7. If serving within 1 - 2 hours, place on counter to set up. If serving later, cover with a large bowl to protect the flavor and refrigerate.

8. Allow to warm for 30 minutes before serving for the creamiest consistency. Just before serving, snip off a tiny corner of the plastic baggie. Pipe a rosette of whipped cream on the end of each slice of pie.*

*Whipped Cream: Recipe makes enough whipped cream for a garnish on the top only. To heavily cover the top of the pie like in restaurants, use 2 half pints (or 16 ounces) of heavy whipping cream and 1/4 cup powdered sugar (unsifted-measure like flour). Whip on medium speed with an electric mixer for 2-3 minutes until stiff peaks form.

If using 16 ounces of heavy whipping cream, make the whipped cream, then add 1 1/3 cup of whipped cream to the pie. Use a pastry bag a large tip to apply the rest of the whipped cream to the top of the pie.

Pie crusts can be baked whenever you have the oven going for something else and frozen for later use. Simply cool and wrap in plastic.

Pumpkin Pie

Makes 2 classic pumpkin pies.

1 - 30 oz can pumpkin
1 1/3 c brown sugar
3 tbsp cornstarch
1 tbsp pumpkin pie spice
1/4 tsp salt

12 oz can evaporated milk
2 tbsp melted butter

2 - 9" pie shells

1. Preheat the oven to 350°.
2. Mix the 1st group of ingredients together in a large bowl.
3. Melt the butter. Stir into the mix along with the evaporated milk.
4. Pour into the pie crust shells. Bake for 70 minutes or until set in the center.

Allow pies to cool at least 30 minutes to fully set.

Pecan Pie

Rich and delicious in every way.

1 1/4 c water
1 c brown sugar
1/4 c cornstarch
1 envelope unflavored gelatin
1/2 tsp salt

3/4 c chopped pecans
1/4 c butter
1 tsp vanilla

3/4 c pecan halves

1 - 9" pie crust

1. Bake the pie crust.
2. Mix the 1st group of ingredients together in a saucepan. Make sure the cornstarch is completely mixed in and smooth before placing over heat.
3. Place over medium heat on the stovetop. Stir until thick and bubbly.
4. Remove from the heat. Stir in the chopped pecans, butter, and vanilla.
5. Pour into the baked pie crust.
6. Decorate the top of the pie with the pecan halves. Start in the center with 5 pecans pointed outward. Fill in pecans in concentric circles moving outward until filled, using halves cut in half around the outside edge.
7. Allow to cool.

Gingerbread Men

These classic cookies can be made crispy or slightly soft depending on how long they are left in the oven.

1/2 c salted butter
1/2 c brown sugar
1/2 c molasses
2 tbsp milk

2 1/2 c flour
1 tsp baking soda (not powder)
1 tsp ground ginger
1/2 tsp cinnamon
1/2 tsp cloves

1. In a large bowl, cream the 1st group of ingredients together using an electric mixer.

2. In a separate bowl, combine the 2nd group of ingredients. Add them to the creamed ingredients and mix until creamy.

3. Roll in plastic wrap and refrigerate until chilled.

4. Preheat the oven to 375°.

5. Roll out the dough on a floured surface to a 1/4" thickness. Cut with a cookie cutter. Place on a greased baking sheet.

6. Bake 5-6 minutes for softer cookies; 8-10 minutes for crisp cookies.

7. Cool on a wire rack. Decorate with icing if desired.

To keep softer cookies fresh, store them in an air tight container as soon as cool. A slice of bread added to the container will help keep them soft for several days.

Gingerbread House

Design your own Christmas cottage with this sheet gingerbread. Or, for a faster method, use graham crackers as your basic building material.

1 c butter
1 c brown sugar
1 c molasses
2 tbsp milk

5 c flour
2 tsp baking soda (not powder)
2 tsp ground ginger
1 tsp ground cinnamon
1 tsp ground cloves

1. Design your house. Draw a template for the walls and roof pieces on light cardboard, such as the inside of a cereal box, and cut out. Or, draw the design on paper and note the measurements for each piece.

2. Preheat the oven to 375°.

3. Cream the 1st group of ingredients. Combine the 2nd group of ingredients, add them to the creamed ingredients and mix until combined. The dough will be very stiff.

4. Roll out the dough onto a floured surface. Kneed a few times to combine all the flour into the dough if needed. Cut the dough in half. Place each half on a greased cookie sheet. Roll out to a 1/4" thickness.

5. Place the cardboard templates on the dough and cut around it with a small sharp knife or a pizza cutter. Or, measure out each piece with a ruler and cut.

6. Bake for 10 minutes. Cool on a wire rack. Separate the pieces where cut.

7. Once cool, use royal icing (page 156) to glue the pieces of the house together, draw on details, and attach candy decorations.

Royal Icing

There are many varieties of frosting that do not require eggs. However the grand standard used by bakers to attach ornamentation is royal icing. This is because of its unique strength, which comes from the addition of egg whites in the mix. This egg-free version offers similar holding power.

1 c powdered sugar
1/4 c corn syrup

1. Mix together with a heavy spoon. This is a really thick icing, so it takes a minute or two with a strong arm to get it to a smooth consistency.

2. If the icing is too thick, a tiny amount of extra corn syrup can be added to achieve a looser consistency.

3. Keep covered until ready to use. Pipe through a pastry bag or strong plastic freezer bag with a tiny hole cut in the corner.

7 Minute Frosting

This bright-white, fat-free frosting, sometimes called marshmallow frosting, can be piled high and it holds its shape well when piped. Traditionally, this glossy fluff is made voluminous by whipping egg whites with a simple sugar syrup.

1 envelope unflavored gelatin
3/4 c cold water

1 c sugar
1/4 tsp salt

1 tsp vanilla

1. Pour the water into a saucepan. Sprinkle the gelatin over the top. Allow to sit for 1 minute before turning on the heat.

2. Add the sugar and salt and place over medium heat. Do not stir while cooking. As soon as bubbles begin to rise, set a timer for two minutes. Allow it to simmer/boil (on a low boil) for 2 minutes. Remove from the heat.

3. Pour into a small mixing bowl. Let cool for 20-30 minutes until lukewarm. Do not cool in the refrigerator as specks of tough gelatin may form.

4. Add the vanilla. Beat on high for 7 minutes until soft peak stage.

5. Use immediately. If delayed and it becomes a little firm, stir well and it will become more spreadable again.

6. Frost the cake. Making small swirls and peaks by lifting the spatula look great. A smooth finish also looks nice. Can be piped through a bag onto cupcakes.

Coloring can be added during the whipping stage. If no color is added, the result will be a glossy bright white.

Makes enough frosting for a 2 layer round cake or 24 cupcakes.

German Chocolate Cake Icing

This caramel-pecan-coconut frosting usually relies on egg yolks to make all this wonderful goo thick enough to hold up on the sides of a cake.

1 14 oz can sweetened condensed milk
1/2 c brown sugar
1 tbsp cornstarch
1 tbsp butter
1 tbsp milk

1 1/2 c flaked coconut
1/2 c chopped pecans
1 tsp vanilla

1. Mix together the first group of ingredients in a heavy saucepan.

2. Melt over low to medium-low heat until it melts and begins to slightly bubble. Allow to simmer for 4-5 minutes stirring frequently.

3. Remove from heat and add the 2nd group of ingredients.

4. Allow to cool before spreading on the cake.

5. Makes enough to cover 2 -9" chocolate cakes stacked with a thin layer in between.

Marshmallow Creme (Fluff)

Who would guess that this common ingredient in many homemade desserts could launch a sneak egg attack?

1 envelope unflavored gelatin
1/2 c water

1 c sugar
1/4 c corn syrup
1/4 tsp salt

1 tsp vanilla

1. Sprinkle the gelatin over 1/2 c cold water in a bowl. Allow to rest 1 minute.

2. Add the sugar, corn syrup and salt. Stir until combined.

3. Pour into a small saucepan. Place over medium heat. Do not stir while cooking.

4. Once it begins to simmer, set a timer for 2 minutes. Let it cook at a low boil for 2 minutes. Turn the heat down a little if it starts to boil rapidly and move up inside the pan.

5. Pour into a mixing bowl. Add the vanilla. Let cool for 15 minutes until the bowl is just warm.

6. Beat on high for 7 minutes until stiff peak stage.

7. Place in an airtight container to store until ready to use.

About the Author

About the Author

Tabitha Elliott discovered a sensitivity to eggs had been plaguing her with health symptoms for years when she was in her early 30's. Due to her busy schedule as a mom with a full-time career, she needed quick and easy recipes with readily available ingredients. When she was unable to find a source of egg-free recipes that tasted good and didn't require a lot of strange ingredients, she began developing recipes of her own. Several years and thousands of test batches later, she decided to combine her recipe box with her long-term desire to write and make the resource she wished she could have found many years ago.

She lives in Missouri with her husband and children. She continues to write and speak on implementing practical solutions for a wide variety of topics.

Attention: Members of the Media, Schools, Businesses, and Non-Profit Organizations

The author is available for interviews and public appearances. Special offers are available for those interested in reselling this cookbook in bulk for educational or promotional purposes.

To inquire, please email littlethingsbooks@gmail.com.

Index

Alphabetical Index

Suggestions?

Do you have ideas for how to improve this cookbook? Suggestions for recipe improvements? Requests for additional recipes to be made egg-free? Do you have other food allergies and can't find a good cookbook?

The author would love to hear from you! Please email her at littlethingbooks@gmail.com or visit Facebook.com/EggFreeCookbook.

The author is available for interviews and speaking engagements. Please contact her at littlethingbooks@gmail.com.

Made in the USA
Coppell, TX
12 July 2020